M000043567

"*Through My Eyes* is an insightful and delightful first person account of the transformation of a rural South Carolina girl into a savvy and sophisticated international metropolitan Atlanta woman. . . . [This book] offers us deep wisdom, wonderful wit, and the persistence, innovation, and courage needed to make what could be mundane into something magnificent!"

—SAMUEL T. GLADDING, PH.D., LPC
Chair & Professor, Department of Counseling
Wake Forest University

"*Through My Eyes* is a funny, witty, and introspective reflection of living in the South. For those like me with Southern roots, it will bring to life your own stories. The book reminds us that life's funniest and most memorable moments are one's spent with family."

—LEONARDO MCCLARTY, IOM
President & CEO, DeKalb Chamber of Commerce
DeKalb County, Georgia

"*Through My Eyes* is . . . full of humorous stories, presented in a clever style. . . . [portraying] a life of love and zest. As [Wynne] shares her memories, she reveals some of the answers to the 'shadows' or the ongoing and eternal questions about human life and values."

—LAURA T. MCCARTY
Vice President, Georgia Humanities Council

"Memoirs like this one provide not just nostalgia and interesting reading for grandchildren—they provide the raw materials that will be used by future historians to delineate the transformation of the Old South to the New South."

—NOEL GRIESE
Editor, *Southern Review of Books*

"In . . . multiple vignettes rendered in an indefatigably breezy style, the author of *Through My Eyes* provides an entertaining chronicle of her long life."

—TOM MACK, PH.D.
G. L. Toole Professor of English, University of South Carolina

"The nostalgia of the South comes alive through . . . a heartfelt memoir that captures the essence of experiencing life as a Southern lady."

—JIMMY BLACKMON
Author, *Southern Roots*

Through My Eyes

Through My Eyes

A Lifetime of Memories—Southern Style

Carolyne Taylor Wynne

Graphite Press

PUBLISHED BY GRAPHITE PRESS

Copyright © 2017 by Carolyne Taylor Wynne

All rights reserved. No part of this book may be used or reproduced without the written permission of the publisher. Graphite Press, Niskayuna, New York.

www.graphitepress.com

ISBN: 978-0-9755810-8-7

LIBRARY OF CONGRESS CATALOGING–IN–PUBLICATION DATA

Names: Wynne, Carolyne Taylor, 1918–2010, author.
Title: Through my eyes : a lifetime of memories—Southern style /
Carolyne Taylor Wynne.
Description: First edition. |
Niskayuna, New York : Graphite Press, 2017. |
Description based on print version record and
CIP data provided by publisher; resource not viewed.
Identifiers: LCCN 2017010018 (print) | LCCN 2017013651 (ebook) |
ISBN 9781938313103 (eBook) |
ISBN 9780975581087 (hardcover : alkaline paper)
Subjects: LCSH: Wynne, Carolyne Taylor, 1918-2010. |
Wynne, Carolyne Taylor, 1918–2010—Travel. |
Women—Southern States—Biography. |
Southern States—Biography. |
Southern States—Social life and customs. |
Ridgeland (S.C.)—Biography. |
Atlanta (Ga.)—Biography.
Classification: LCC CT275.W956 (ebook) |
LCC CT275.W956 A3 2017 (print) | DDC
920.72—dc23
LC record available at https://lccn.loc.gov/2017010018

FIRST EDITION

Contents

Part One
Life in South Carolina – Country Girl

CHAPTER 1
Life on the Farm

CHAPTER 2
Life in the New House

CHAPTER 3
Life as a Teenager

CHAPTER 4
Life of Adjustments

Part Two
Life in Atlanta – Southern Lady

CHAPTER 5
Life With My Family

CHAPTER 6
Life With My Friends

Part Three
Life With a Passport – International Traveler

Part Four
Life Among Relatives – Legacy of Memories

Afterword
Life Through My Eyes – My Reflections

Acknowledgments

A special thanks to…

— my creative writing instructor, Doris Turrentine, for inspiring me to write of my past.

— my youngest daughter, Terry, for helping me organize these memoirs and for putting them on the computer.

— my family and friends who helped me to have an interesting and exciting life.

A Welcome Message

These memoirs are written as seen Through My Eyes. They begin with a large farm, a large family, and a large number of early memories. Enjoy reading about our inconveniences of yesteryear and our joys and conveniences of today.

Carolyne Taylor Wynne

Part One

Life in South Carolina – Country Girl

Carolyne, the country girl, at the farmhouse.

The Low Country

U NLESS you have…

— dug a hole in the ground, placed hot glowing hickory coals under pigs, continually basted them with a special barbecue sauce all through the night, and eaten these succulent barbecue sandwiches;

— seen sugar cane brought from the fields to a mill where mules were used to turn the wheels and grind the juices into a big barrel;

— vied with the bumblebees, dodging between the mules, to get a glass of sugar cane juice;

— smelled the rich cane juice cooking in a large boiler to just the right thickness for syrup;

— reached for the golden grapes on the very top of a scuppernong arbor;

— smashed a watermelon in the field, ate the luscious fruit with your fingers, and felt the sweet juice sliding down your chin;

— timidly tried to milk a cow, often missing the bucket;

— put worms on your own fish hook to catch fresh pike and bream from a pond;

— pulled peanuts from a vine, washed and washed them, and waited impatiently for the wash pot to cook them to a just-right salted tenderness;

— picked wild blackberries and huckleberries for cobblers, jams, and jellies;

— plucked fresh corn from the field and eaten it 15 minutes later;

— gathered eggs from the henhouse just before cooking them for breakfast;

— gone to your own smokehouse to get a home-cured ham to bake;

— sat in the porch rocking chair and shelled beans or peas;

— taken a turn at the hand-cranked churn to make straw-
berry custard ice cream;
— roasted a turkey or fried a chicken from your own chicken
yard;

...then you've never enjoyed real Southern living on a South
Carolina farm in the Low Country!

Chapter 1
Life on the Farm

All About Me

YES, I was a tomboy! We lived on a large farm less than two miles from Ridgeland, a small, small town in lower South Carolina. I can remember my mother and father drove a Model T Ford. It had a running board and had to be hand-cranked. I had an older sister, Helen, who thought I was a brat; an older brother, Vernon; and three younger brothers, Gray, Jimmy, and Kent. I was not allowed the same freedom as my brothers.

There were few toys, but we didn't miss them because we had never had any. None of the other kids had any either. We made a pretend store with leaves, berries, old cans, bottles, and bottle tops. Our money was composed of broken glass—blue or green glass was especially valuable. Usually, there was a ball and a bat that was made from a tree limb.

I resorted to climbing trees, riding horses, fishing in the pond, and taking long walks in the woods, sometimes joining my brothers in their pastimes. We would make mud pies, play ball, jump rope, play hopscotch, climb trees, ride the pony, and there was always a swing. I don't remember life being dull. These were such carefree times.

I knew where to find the early violets, the wild Easter lilies, the luscious huckleberries, and the high-bush blackberries. Mulberry trees grew along the path from the house to the barn. Great quantities of the mulberries fell to the ground when ripe. I couldn't avoid them as I walked along the path. I hated the feeling of the squishy berries between my toes and under my bare feet.

I remember the early inconveniences. Our telephone was on a party line. We had no electricity so we had to use kerosene lamps for lighting, fireplaces for heat, and a wood-burning stove in the kitchen for cooking. We had no flush toilets and no running water.

The outdoor privy was always a good ways from the house, around the grape arbor beyond the fig trees. We used an old Sears Roebuck catalog for toilet paper. I've heard of people using corncobs, but we never did that!

We had to go out of the farmhouse down the long back porch to get to the kitchen and dining room. A pump for water was on the porch. A basin, soap, and towel to wash the face and hands were beside the pump. Water from this pump was used for all household needs including drinking, cooking, and bathing.

In the summertime, for bathing, the water was heated in kettles, then brought to a claw-footed bathtub in a small bathroom that had no source of heat. Needless to say, the barest of necessities was used in that small room.

In the wintertime, on Saturday nights, a large washtub was brought into the bedroom and filled with hot water. It was placed in front of the fireplace, where a big fire was built. We were bathed and our hair washed and dried in front of the fireplace, put in clean, warm pajamas, and snuggled into bed under many quilts.

When I was just four years old, I remember the day I slipped my mother's umbrella out, climbed a ladder to the top of the car shed, opened the umbrella, and bravely parachuted to the ground. Luckily, the shed was surrounded by deep, loose sand—but even that didn't keep my feet from tingling for two days. I never parachuted again until I was twenty—at Coney Island.

I vividly remember the day I was burned. It happened in the kitchen. Four-year-old me had been playing under the ironing board where the cook, Marie, had been ironing. Then she began making supper. She had finished frying meat and went to pour the grease into a can. I stood up and upset the frying pan, spilling the hot grease all over my head, face, and left arm. I began to scream and didn't stop until an hour later when the doctor came and gave me a sedative. My beautiful long, golden curls were cut—it was months later before all had healed. The hair never grew back on the spot that was burned on my head. I was so fortunate that my face wasn't scarred. I still remember the pain and the *screaming*!

I remember the birthday when I was six years old. I thought I was the luckiest little girl in the world. My presents were a pink toothbrush, my own toothpaste, crayons, a rough-sheeted red horse tablet, and a pencil with a big eraser. I was so pleased! I couldn't wait to take the pencil to my Grandfather Taylor's office to use his nice pencil sharpener.

Although that birthday was my very last at the farmhouse, I have lots of tales to tell...

The Farm

The farmhouse is where we lived until I was six years old. The farm itself consisted of over a thousand acres including the huge barns and stables and lots and sheds and kennels and pastures and fields and crops and grape arbors and a large vegetable garden and fig trees and pecan trees and moss-covered oaks and an orchard and a sugar cane mill and a chicken house and a smokehouse and a duck pond and a fishpond. My mother's sisters always referred to our farm as a plantation.

The land was used for different things at different times. There was a time when cotton was the main crop and a time when my father did truck farming. Boxcar loads of cucumbers, cantaloupes, watermelons, green beans, and new potatoes were shipped up north. The earlier in a season they were shipped, the more money they earned. Some of the land was always used to plant grains and other crops to make hay and food for the animals.

On another part of the land, my father built a duck pond and a fishpond. The ducks would fly down from Canada and rest for a while at the duck pond before flying on to Florida for the winter.

There was a wooden fence that surrounded a large barn as well as the lot. The loft of the barns and sheds were filled with bales of hay. In the lot, there were wooden troughs that had to be filled with water and food for the animals. We had mules, horses, and cows in the lots and barns; hogs in the pastures; a Brahma bull for crossbreeding; goats to eat the underbrush; and even cats to catch the barn rats.

On hot summer days, we children loved to ride on the back of the mule-drawn wagon that took feed to the hogs. We would sit and bounce with our bare feet hanging down. The wagon would have to pass through a branch of water. It was just deep enough to come halfway up our legs. This cold water would cool our hot and dusty feet.

There was no one who could compete with my father's hog calling. He would stand at the edge of a pasture and begin calling, "Hoooog pig, hoooog pig!" And the hogs and pigs would come running from all around to get their food. Sometimes, they would be waiting by the fence at five o'clock, the time they were usually fed.

There were several large, sweet, fig trees, my mother's favorite, but not mine. We also had an orchard containing plum trees and peach trees, good for preserves, pies, and cobblers, and sometimes peach ice cream.

There was an abundance of blackberries and huckleberries for the picking. Before we began to pick, we placed old, runny, nylon stockings on our hands and arms to prevent the briers from hurting us. These berries were used to make jams and jellies as well as pies, cakes, and cobblers. My favorite was blackberry cobbler, and it still is today.

We had scuppernong grape arbors. I remember going out in the early morning or late afternoon and finding the ripe grapes. Thank goodness we had two large arbors. When the grapes were ripe, we always had lots of visitors!

Barbecues were special times for our family and friends. Several pigs were killed and cleaned, a pit dug, and hickory wood used for a fire. Once the wood burned to embers, it was placed under the meat, which was continually basted and cooked slowly for about 24 hours. My mother was very adept at making Brunswick stew and barbecue sauce to accompany the barbecue pork, buns, corn on the cob, cole slaw, sliced tomatoes, lettuce, potato salad, gallons of sweet tea, and for dessert, brownies and cookies. If you were lucky, you would get to take home tomorrow's lunch. When we had a barbecue, we always had lots of visitors!

In the fall, as the weather began to turn cold, the sugar cane was cut and brought to the mill in back of our house. A pole was hitched to a poor mule that just went round and round and round, turning two big wheels, squeezing the juice from the cane into a barrel. We had to vie with the bumblebees, and dodge the mule to get a glass of that cold, sweet juice. The juice was emptied into a large boiler with fire underneath it, and the juice cooked and cooked and cooked until it became syrup. My mother would go out and decide when the syrup was cooked to just the right consistency, not too thin and not too thick. If it was too thick, it would be sugary. Company, neighbors, and friends never failed to take home a jar of the fresh, still-warm syrup. When we made cane syrup, we always had lots of visitors!

When the weather turned cold, cold, it was time for hog killing. The meat was cut into hams and bacon to be cured. Sausages and liver pudding were made and lard rendered. Our favorite breakfast was the pig's feet—boiled, chilled, sliced in two, dipped in cornmeal, and fried.

I remember the Christmas at the farm when we were very small. We each received a chair—Helen, a rocking chair with arms; Vernon, a smaller one; me, a rocking chair without arms; Gray, a small folding chair. I remember Christmas dinner with the 25-pound turkey and the homemade cranberry relish. When we had Christmas dinner, we always had lots of visitors!

No matter what we had to eat, we always had lots of visitors!

The Farm Workers

On the farm was a gate in front of the road that led into the fields and pastures. I remember the big bell that stood by the gate. All work and life seemed to be determined by the ringing of the bell. The bell was rung three times a day: at sunup, startin' time for the "hands" to begin work in the fields; at noon, eatin' time; and at sundown, quittin' time. It was loud enough to be heard by the more than two-dozen black families that worked for my father and lived in the cabins on the farm.

Friday was the name of the black man who was in charge of the farm. Marie, his daughter, was our cook. There was Clara, who came frequently to clean windows and do the heavy cleaning; Aunt Minnie, who came each Monday to pick up our dirty clothes to launder; and Aunt Maria, who was a midwife and came to help when mother had a baby. Then there was Monday, the head ditch digger, who also worked in the road construction area.

We children were not allowed to go to the cabins of the black families that lived on the farm, but we didn't always obey. I could not understand this, for one did our washing and ironing, one did our cleaning, and another our cooking. I remember their cabins were wallpapered with old newspapers to keep out the cold wind. They would give us hot corn pones and sweet potatoes cooked in their fireplaces. Their sweet potatoes were sugary like candy, the best I've ever tasted, and so hot we would have to pass them from one hand to the other.

The black people who lived in the cabins on the farm would often congregate to sorta visit and sing. They would clap their hands and stomp their feet to make their own music. They called these gatherings, "shoutings." They would shout their hymns in time with their self-made music. This was one of their favorite ways of bringing joy into their lives.

From our house, we could sometimes hear the bell as well as the shoutings.

The CEO

Charley was a black man who worked for my father. All the black families living on the farm seemed to look up to this black, black man with the white, white teeth and the most engaging, smiling face. He seemed to be the inspiration to get the workers up when the farm bell rang at sunrise. According to the season, some were to plow, to hoe, pick vegetables, dig potatoes, pick cotton, or care for the animals. I guess you could call Charley, the farm's CEO.

In addition to owning the farm, my father also was a road contractor, who built many of the original dirt roads in South Carolina. When the roads were being built many miles from home, Charley was always there, keeping the men digging ditches, working long hours, then bringing the men home on Saturday with pockets jingling with money. I guess Charley was thought of as the construction crew's CEO.

Charley could neither read nor write, but wanted to communicate with his girlfriend—our cook, Marie. He hired my fourteen-year-old brother, Vernon, to write his love letters. When asked what he wished to say in the letters, he would answer, "Write 'Dear Marie,' and tell her I for love her."

"What next?" my brother would ask.

"Tell her I for love her again, love and kisses, signed Charley."

The strange thing is that the lack of words was very unusual for Charley, who was very glib of tongue. He bragged about the many times he was stopped for speeding or other misdemeanors when transporting the men. He would talk the patrolman out of giving him a ticket, sometimes, even persuading the patrolman to give them a few dollars for snacks.

Charley was also the preacher for his church. I only heard him preach one time. There was a special occasion when the bishop was to be present. My father was asked to give the accreditation for Charley. My brother, Vernon, and I accompanied my father. It was an all-day service, but we only stayed for the special portion.

The church could not hold all the people. There was the whole black community, including our farm workers. Gone were the sweat, the dirt, the brogans, the aprons, the overalls—replaced by colorful dresses, ties, hats, and *Hoyt's Cologne*! On that hot, sultry, July Sunday, there was never a letup in the swishing of the cardboard fans, donated by the funeral home. The heat was so stifling, we had difficulty breathing.

Then Charley, resplendent in his suit, tie, red vest, and top hat, went to the pulpit. First, he called upon my father to give him the accreditation. Next, he began to read the scripture with his Bible upside down. He must have had an excellent memory for he didn't miss a word.

With much clapping and loud amens, I guess the people of the church considered Charley God's CEO!

Aunt Phoebe

I remember Aunt Phoebe, a shriveled, wizened, stooped, tiny, old black woman of indeterminate age. My estimate was that she was more than a hundred years old. The hump on her back made her look less than four feet tall. I was four years old and deathly afraid of her. I just knew she was a "witch."

She would pass by our farmhouse most every day. She lived in one of the many cabins scattered about the farm in which the hands that worked for my father lived. Aunt Phoebe would be dressed in many layers of dark clothing, the hem of her skirt almost touching the ground. Her brogan shoes with untied laces seemed to be too big for her tiny feet, causing her to shuffle along as she walked, hardly lifting her feet from the ground. Her lower lip protruded and she constantly spat because she dipped snuff.

She always carried a crocus sack hung across her shoulders, much like a large tote bag of today. It was so lumpy-looking, I wondered if it contained poisonous herbs, frogs, live chickens, or maybe even a wiggly snake.

My older siblings would run out and taunt her. She would look at them with her beady, red eyes, shaking her head so hard that her head rag would almost fall off, saying, "I'm gonna put bad 'mouf' on you young'uns." Then my siblings would join me in my hiding place.

Sometimes, at dusk, we would see her passing by to return home—a trifle more dusty, her steps much slower, with the crocus sack bulging with strange, new lumps.

I never found out what the crocus sack contained!

Cotton Pickin'

It was a good year for growing cotton on the farm. We watched the cotton pickers with their crocus sacks in one of the fields across the road from the farmhouse. The headman weighed each bag of cotton and kept account of how much each person picked. The pickers emptied their full bags into a mule-drawn wagon, then resumed picking cotton again. When the wagon was full, it was emptied, and returned to the field. At the end of each day, we watched the workers receiving payment for the cotton they had picked.

When I was four years old and my older brother Vernon was seven, we decided we wanted to pick cotton too. So we each found a crocus sack, went to the field, and began picking. The cotton hurt our tender little fingers as we pulled it out of the burrs. After the cotton pickers watched us struggling to even carry sacks larger than we were, they would give us a handful of cotton out of their own sack.

We worked a couple of hours that afternoon. When quittin' time came, the headman weighed our bags of cotton and paid us for our afternoon of hard work.

I had earned five cents!

My First Surgical Experience

Because Ridgeland, the small town nearest our farm, had a population of less than a thousand, there was no hospital. Once a year, several surgeons would come from Charleston, South Carolina, and have a tonsil clinic. The best facility the town could provide was the county courthouse, a much-used building in many ways. Most rooms even had brass spittoons for tobacco chewers. The users often missed their aim.

The damp Low Country seemed to encourage swollen glands, infected tonsils, and fever. It was decided it was time for my seven-year-old brother Vernon and four-year-old me to have our tonsils removed.

The courthouse was readied. Desks and chairs were removed from several rooms, cots were set up, and court cases were cancelled for several days. Yes, the spittoons were also removed.

We, soon to become patients, along with our mothers, were herded into a large courtroom. One by one, we were called to the operating room. After several hours, I heard, "Next, Vernon Taylor." My little heart stood still for I knew the next name called would be mine. It was hardly five minutes before a nurse took my hand and we entered a closed door.

The ether odor was overwhelming, and there on the other operating table was my brother. A nurse was holding something that looked like a large strainer with a cloth in it over his nose. The doctor was holding a knife-like instrument.

My mouth came open and the screams could be heard in the judge's chambers. Leaving my poor brother alone, his nurse quickly transferred the strainer to my nose. His doctor held me down as my team took over. The last thing I saw was my doctor picking up a knife.

Several hours later, I awoke on a cot next to my brother on one side and an adult male on the other. I did not care for the ice cream that was offered. However, I had no choice about the Milk of Magnesia. A nurse came around with the largest tablespoon I had ever seen, especially with my swollen mouth. We each had the same spoon wiped on the same towel after each use. Finally, it was morning, and we were allowed to go home.

To this day, I still have a fear of doctors and hospitals!

The Roller Coaster

There was not a great deal of ready cash when I was a small child. We were only given a penny each to put into the collection plate at Sunday school. But each year, when the circus and the fair came to Savannah, Georgia, and when the circus and the state fair were in Columbia, South Carolina, my father and mother would let us skip school and take us for a day.

You had to be in school to be a big kid. When I was still a little kid, I remember the roller coaster. I was the third child of six. My sister, Helen, was ten; my brother, Vernon, was eight; and I was only five. I was really too young for a big roller coaster, which was my siblings' first choice to ride. But, at my insistence, being my father's favorite child, he bought tickets for all three of us.

It was my first ride on a roller coaster. I sat in the middle, the workers fastened the bar, and I held on as the roller coaster climbed the first hill. When we reached the top and I looked down, I panicked, crying and screaming. "Stop, stop, let me off! I'm going to fall out! Please, please stop! I'll never get on this ride again! I hate it!" All the while, my sister and brother were laughing joyously, having a great time. I didn't stop crying and yelling until the ride was over.

The minute we were let off, Helen and Vernon ran to my father, begging to ride again. I told him I wanted to go too.

"No, no, no, we don't want Carolyne to go. She'll cry and scream. She hates it," they said.

My father, wanting to please his youngest daughter, told them if they wished to ride again, they would have to take their little sister. So, with me in the middle and the bar fastened, we began to move. My brother and sister laughed excitedly. Even as we reached the top of the first climb, my tears began to flow. My eyes were wide with terror, my mouth flew open, and the screaming began!

The next year, I had started to school when we rode the roller coaster. I squeezed my eyes shut and held on so tightly, there were blisters on my hands. But I didn't cry. I didn't scream.

I was a big kid now!

The Red Stuff

My little two-year-old brother, Gray, had a kiddie car that he was not allowed to ride because the handlebars had come off, leaving two iron rods exposed.

One day, I thought it would be fun to ride the little car, but first, I had to get it down the back steps. I decided to ride it down the steps. The next thing I knew, I found myself upside down on the ground with "red stuff" gushing out of my arm from having fallen on the iron rods.

I climbed up those steps and went inside to find something to wipe the "red stuff" off my arm. When a washcloth became saturated, I found a towel. When the towel became saturated, I found a sheet and hid inside of a closet. I just knew I'd get a spanking for riding the broken car.

My older sister, Helen, saw a trail of blood leading from the steps into the house, but couldn't find where it came from. She started calling and opening doors and finally, there was little five-year-old me curled up in a corner of the closet with the "red stuff" covering half of the sheet. She gasped and immediately called my mother. It only took a quick glance before my mother was ringing up the operator to call the doctor to come quickly.

To remind me I lost so much "red stuff" from my daring ride that I almost bled to death, I still have a two-inch scar on my arm!

Jack

I remember the time my father bought a pony for my brother Vernon when he was eight years old, just three years older than I. We all, including my father but not my mother, took a short ride on Jack, a Shetland pony. Some weeks later, Vernon announced that while riding Jack, he had jumped a ditch down the road, on the right side of the woods, before you reach the highway.

I persuaded him that it was my time to ride. Down the road I went, to the right side of the woods, before you reach the highway, spying a two-foot wide, three-foot deep ditch. I said, "There it is, Jack," kicking my five-year-old heels in his side, holding on for dear life as Jack began to run. But, Jack had an idea of his own. He stopped dead still, dumping me into the ditch. Then, he turned around and ran home.

I climbed out of that ditch, hurting not only from the fall, but from my pride as well. I walked home slowly. I needed time to dry my tears before I had to listen to my siblings' loud laughter!

Easter at the Farm

I remember Easter time at the farm. Very often, we would set our own traps and capture a real bunny for Easter. When we were small, we were allowed to color and place a decal on our own egg and keep it for ourselves. My mother helped us dye the rest of the eggs for our egg hunt.

I remember searching for eggs early on Easter morning. Dozens of brightly colored eggs were hidden in the backyard around and about the woodpile, the fig trees, and the grape arbors, for there were no grassy lawns at the farm, only black dirt and sand.

We always had the Easter egg hunt before breakfast. The early mornings were cool and very damp with dew. After finding the eggs, we would go back inside. The big wood stove in the kitchen would make the dining room adjacent to it warm and cozy. The cook would have the coffee, grits, bacon, and toast ready and waiting for us—they smelled so good! We were allowed to have coffee, that is, milk with a couple of tablespoons of coffee in it with some sugar. The eggs that we had found completed the breakfast.

Now, my father loved boiled eggs. One time, I saw him eat

a dozen of them for breakfast. He would take a sharp-ended egg and hit either end of our egg. If he cracked our egg, it belonged to him. This was called pipping, and he always seemed to win.

After breakfast, we hurried to put on our new Easter finery to be on time for Sunday school and church before returning home to eat Easter dinner about one o'clock.

There was a whole baked ham, glazed and studded with cloves, not to mention the fried chicken, the tossed salad with avocados, the ginger ale congealed salad, the vegetables, and our favorite dessert, floating island. Counting the visiting relatives, there would be at least 20 of us. Most of the time, the men ate at the dining table, the children in the kitchen, and the women had to eat last.

At the end of the day, the remaining Easter eggs were gathered to make deviled eggs, creamed eggs on toast, and egg sandwiches.

No matter how much we practiced, none of us were ever able to pip like my father!

Chapter 2
Life in the New House

More About Me

JUST before I started school for the first time, we moved into a new house less than a mile from the farmhouse. We did not take the old, beat-up furniture, but I did take and keep all my childhood memories of the farm.

At the new house, we were the first in the county to have electric lights and running water. People from all over the county came to see the modern conveniences. I would proudly run ahead of them, stand on my tiptoes, and push the switch to show off the electric lights in the four bedrooms with a fireplace in each; in the living room with French doors, a chandelier, and a large, log-burning fireplace; in the dining room that also had a chandelier and a fireplace; in the kitchen that had a wood-burning stove; and even in the bathroom that had hot and cold running water. We always had *lots* of visitors!

Not only did my family move to a new house, but we also had three new school buildings. Helen began high school in the two-story building; Vernon began school in the grammar school building; and I began 1st grade in the third building. Up to this time, Helen and Vernon had attended school in a one-room schoolhouse with a potbellied stove for heat. Our three new school buildings had radiators.

The first day of school came and I was on that school bus. The bus went very slowly because of the elderly bus, the elderly bus driver, and the deep, sandy, unpaved road. About half a mile from the schoolhouse, the big boys would hop out of the bus and be sitting on the school steps, smirking, when the bus arrived, much to the chagrin of the driver. But next year, we would have a new bus, a new bus driver, and a new paved road.

We soon opened a country store, much like the ones owned by both of my grandfathers. We also sold gasoline and kerosene. Cotton was the prevalent crop at that time, so my father built a cotton gin and then a gristmill, which not only ground grits, but also meal. Besides all of this and the farm, he still continued building roads.

The older I became, the more I grew, the more tales I have to tell…

Guns and Shooting

Our favorite Sunday afternoon pastime was having our father teach us how to shoot a gun. Our targets were tin cans on a fence post. My father was an excellent shot and he wanted us to become one too. He always kept guns not only in the house, but also in his pickup.

One late afternoon when I was with him in his pickup, he thought he saw a covey of quail on the edge of the woods. So he told nine-year-old me to walk toward the large bushes, make a lot of noise, and flush them out. Well, they fooled him! They let me get within two feet of them and flushed out right in my face. He thought they would fly in the opposite direction. He began to shoot over my head. He killed plenty of birds for breakfast the next day, but his youngest daughter, me, didn't care for any at that time.

Today, I'm still afraid of our feathered friends!

Dogs and Hunting

I remember my father riding a horse and being pretty good at it. There were coveys of quail and dove on the farm as well as deer and fox. My father loved to hunt: fox hunting, deer hunting, and duck and bird shooting. But what he liked the best was fox hunting.

He kept about 20 dogs in a kennel, with a man just to take care of them. He could tell the barks of each of his dogs, but it seemed that when he went fox hunting on Saturday night, one would always get lost. So, on Sunday afternoons, he would load all six of us children and my mother in the car, drive where there were no roads, and blow his fox horn until he found his lost dog. Jimmy and Kent, the two youngest boys, would sit in the front seat with mother and dad. Then, Vernon and Helen and Gray and I, *and the foxhound*, would be in the backseat.

We had about five or six cows that were milked, not only for family use, but also to feed the many dogs my father owned. The milk for the dogs was allowed to sour and clabber, then the cream was skimmed and made into butter. We children requested that the cream also be skimmed from the milk that we drank, although the milk was still rich even after the cream was taken off. I guess that was why we were all so skinny as kids.

Of course, the dogs were lean too, even though the cook baked large dishpans full of cornbread to feed them each day. Even though money was scarce, once a week, salmon was bought for them. My father was not going to have fat dogs!

One winter, my father even bought boots for his dogs so their feet wouldn't be frostbitten.

The dogs got boots, but we children didn't!

The Piano and Me

In the 2nd grade, my mother insisted that I take piano lessons. I just hated to practice on the piano when there were so many interesting things to do and always something new to discover.

I longed to be outside playing with my siblings, climbing trees, riding and jumping ditches with the pony, picking blackberries, finding the violets hiding in the woods in the springtime, eating the blueberries at the edge of the field that left telltale color on your teeth in the summer, and gathering the most colorful leaves in the fall.

How could learning to strike the right keys on a piano compare with the adventures of discovery?

Tickling the ivories must be for adults!

My Favorite Teacher

When I was seven years old, in the 2nd grade, I was utterly enraptured with my teacher. Miss Stanmeyer was a lovely, young blonde with beautiful dark-blue eyes and a happy smile. I was obsessed to know how old she was. Very often, I rudely asked her to tell us her age. Finally, she found a solution to my brashness. Going to the blackboard, she wrote an equation much like this:

$$9 \times 4 + 10 \div 2 \times 6 \div 3 - 24 = ?$$

"When you solve the problem, you will have the answer," we were told. This was beyond the level we had reached. But, she had misjudged my advancement in math. I was so smug. I wouldn't share the answer with my classmates. She was 22.

Our home was about two miles from the school. About once a week, Miss Stanmeyer would call my mother and ask if I could visit with her after school and she would take me home.

While the teacher graded papers and prepared her lesson plans, she would let me arrange her jewelry and read her books. It was from these books she chose the stories she read to the class. Before she took me home, we would always go the drug store for a Cherry Coke. After Christmas, a dark-haired, charming young man began to pick us up and join us for the Coke.

One afternoon toward the end of the year, they asked to come in and talk to my mother. After school was out, they were going to get married, and wanted me to be the flower girl in their wedding! My mother painstakingly began to make my little dress. She used lots of tucks and scallops with lace and embroidered pink flowers. I felt so special as I walked down the aisle in my new dress and Mary Janes with a basket full of pink rose petals.

My beloved Miss Stanmeyer and her beloved husband moved away and I never saw them again.

But, I still have the little dress!

My Favorite Game

Around the 3rd grade in school, at recess, a group would hold hands and form a circle to play games like "Farmer in the Dell" and "Drop the Handkerchief." My favorite was "Marching Round the Level." We would count out, "Eeny, meeny, miny, moe," to find out who was going to be "*It.*"

It stood in the middle of the circle while the group marched around *It* singing, "We're marching round the level, we're marching round the level, we're marching round the level, 'til we have gained this day."

The group stood still while singing the second stanza, "Go forth and face your lover," ending with, " 'til we have gained this day." *It* stands in front of one of the opposite sex while the group sings the third stanza, "I measure my love to show you." *It* measures the amount of love with arms outspread.

During the fourth stanza, "I kneel because I love you," *It* kneels before the chosen one. The fifth stanza was, "One kiss before I leave you." *It* had to carry out each motion in each stanza. *It* then joins the circle and the lover becomes *It*.

I was so scared that no one would choose me, but more afraid that they would. Then, that cute little blonde, blue-eyed Alfred, who I had a crush on, was standing in front of me. And when he gave me that wet smack on the cheek, I was so embarrassed, but so pleased.

Carolyne had just had her first kiss!

A Visit to Jacksonville

Before my youngest brother, Kent, the 6th child in the family, was born in October, it was decided the four eldest children, Helen, Vernon, Carolyne, and Gray, would go and visit my Grandmother Gray and Aunt Gladys in Jacksonville, Florida, for the month of August to give my mother a break. We ranged in age from about six to fifteen. We took a young black girl with us as a sorta nursemaid and to help with the laundry and dishwashing.

We went by train from Ridgeland, South Carolina. It was around thirty miles to Savannah, Georgia. A large lunch, enough to last the five of us until we reached our destination, was prepared and placed in shoeboxes: fried chicken, deviled eggs, sandwiches, and cookies. Before we reached Savannah, all the food was gone.

Living in the country made city life fascinating to us. We loved going to the park, getting frosted root beers, riding the streetcars, going to the beaches, and shopping in the big stores.

My grandmother and aunt lived in an apartment house. Their across-the-hall neighbor had a maid who wore a black uniform with a fancy little white apron and cap. Twice a week, I would hear a loud, whirring noise coming from across the hall. The maid would be using a big Hoover vacuum cleaner that sounded like a bulldozer. This machine was the most fascinating thing to me—the way it would eat the dust and lint and sand and whatever. Sometimes, the maid would let me push it.

When my parents came for us at the end of the month, my Grandmother Gray asked what we would like to take home with us.

I immediately answered, "The Hoover vacuum cleaner from across the hall!"

The May Festival

At the school's May Festival one year, I was selected to be one of the dancers around the Maypole. I was ecstatic! My mother and other relatives were in the crowd that was watching.

We had no problem dancing in and out winding up the ribbons, for we had practiced well. It was decided that we would also unwind the ribbons. Now, no one applauded as we perfectly wound the ribbons around the pole. But as soon as we became frustrated and messed up the unwinding, the clapping began. The tangled mess of ribbons delighted the crowd. They seemed to enjoy our embarrassment and applauded even louder.

The applause at the May Festival never again reached the peak that it did in the year of "Our Tangled Embarrassment!"

High Tea

The family of my best friend sold their plantation to a multimillionaire from New York. He restored the antebellum home, built a racetrack for his racehorses, built kennels for the hunting dogs, and also a dock for their yacht as the house was on a river. A new home was built nearby for my friend's family because her father was retained as manager of the estate.

Twice a year, to this South Carolina home, the new owner

would bring some of his New York staff—the English butler and housekeeper, the chef, and the French maids. Every other day, florist trucks from Savannah, Georgia, delivered fresh flowers to the house. This was my first experience with this type of wealth.

When I was ten years old, I often spent weekends with my chum. Sometimes, we would confiscate the expensive bars of soap that were thrown out after one use. Occasionally, we were allowed to walk the horses to cool them down after they had been running. How exciting for us to get to ride real racehorses!

One day, when the estate owner was away, the housekeeper invited my friend and me to high tea at three o'clock on Saturday afternoon. We shampooed our hair, put on our Sunday school dresses, and our shiny Mary Janes. We arrived both thrilled and scared!

The butler ushered us into the parlor. A beautiful silver tea service was set up. The housekeeper performed the same ceremony she used for the owner, his family, and their guests—the rinsing with boiling water for heating the teapot, the careful measuring of the tea, the timing of the brewing, and then the pouring of the golden hot liquid. We were asked if we would like sugar—one lump or two? Lemon or cream? She showed us how to hold the delicate, thin China cups and the proper use of the lovely linen napkins. She taught us to take very small bites of the dainty, crustless watercress and cucumber sandwiches. Then, she served us English scones with clotted cream and jam.

Yes, we crooked our little fingers and pretended we were royalty!

The 7th Grade

There's nothing like being twelve years old. You think the world was made just for you, and you know everything about it. My 7th grade class was very active in sports and all phases of school life. We thought the teacher, Mrs. Givens, was ancient, too old to be teaching. She was in her early thirties.

I was prodded by the class to be their spokesperson, which often kept me in trouble. Mrs. Givens, using me as an example of disciplinary action, would send me to the principal's office. His punishment would usually be memorizing poetry: Longfellow, Emerson, Tennyson, and others. I still remember snatches of "Under a Spreading Chestnut Tree," "Abou Ben Adhem," "By the shining Big-Sea-Water," "A Rose is a Rose," and "Dark Brown is the River."

The principal of this small-town school wore many hats. He taught 6th and 7th grade math, coached all sports, as well as performed his "principaling" duty. I was kind of a godsend to him. Before long, I was correcting his papers and filling out report cards.

One day, I must have been exasperating. Mrs. Givens again sent me to the principal's office saying that I was the "disturbing element" of the class. This day, I was allowed to do something special. The 2nd grade teacher had an emergency, so I was sent to teach her 2nd grade class for two hours until school was out for the day. The 2nd graders didn't realize I wasn't an adult because I was already 5 feet 7 inches tall. I knew I had to keep them busy. I knew nothing of lesson plans. I started off with a spelling bee, then read them a story, and had them draw pictures to depict the story. I still had 30 minutes to go. I saw the world globe. I loved geography and told them of the different countries, their cultures, and people.

Toward the end of the school year, the class bully threw an eraser narrowly missing the teacher's head. No one would own up to the deed, so Mrs. Givens announced that the whole class would stay in after school. This meant everyone would miss a school-sports-championship game. I raised my hand saying I had thrown the eraser. Thoroughly exasperated with me, stating that I was the "disturbing element" of the school, Mrs.

Givens sent me again to the principal's office.

Twelve year olds didn't receive much mail, but during the summer vacation, a letter arrived addressed and written to me in beautiful script. I kept this letter a long time.

It began, "Dear Little Disturbing Element, I knew all along you were not the troublemaker," and was signed, "Lovingly, Mrs. Givens."

Christmastime

By the time December came, I would have spotted the lowest growing mistletoe, the holly with the reddest berries, and the most beautiful pine tree on our farm. We used our very own homegrown greenery and tree for decorating at Christmas. My mother would wrap an icicle on the long pine needles of our Christmas tree. One Christmas, we clipped small candleholders onto each branch—how dangerous, but beautiful when the candles were lit!

The fruitcakes were baked before Thanksgiving in large, round pans as well as some small, loaf ones—some dark fruitcakes and some white fruitcakes. They tasted even better at Christmastime.

Sometimes, my mother's sister Gladys and her husband; my mother's brothers, Ruth and Lewis; and my Grandmother Gray joined us at Christmas. That meant lots more presents under the tree! The men went deer hunting and bird shooting. There was always plenty of venison, doves, and quail. We would have the doves and quail for breakfast.

There was one very special Christmas when we gave my brothers, Kent and Jimmy, a pellet pistol. As soon as my mother left the room, all of us took turns shooting it. It was not very strong, but to my mother's dismay, strong enough to shoot the ornaments off the Christmas tree from the far side of the room.

We all got caught, but no one confessed—not even my dad!

New Year's Eve

I remember seeing my first New Year's come in. I was twelve years old.

We went to bed early and arose early on the farm. There was no television and worse than that, no central heat. Everyone but me went to bed at ten o'clock on this New Year's Eve. I put another log on the fire, found a quilt to cuddle up in, and turned on the radio.

I listened to the big-name bands from different cities. Still, the hands of the clock barely crawled around. My eyelids became heavy, but I was determined to see the new year come bursting in.

Finally, there was Guy Lombardo's "Auld Lang Syne" from Times Square, and then a countdown. The radio became noisy and very loud. Not so in our house. There was complete silence. The fire had gone out.

No doors flying open; no Father Time departing; no toddling, diapered, new baby entering—just one cold, sleepy, shivering, disillusioned little girl!

Chapter 3
Life as a Teenager

Still More About Me

MY brothers learned to drive from operating the farm equipment. When I was ten years old, my older sister Helen taught me to drive, but not well enough. Overconfident me was driving too fast to turn in at our house and hit a pine tree. My father said nothing to me; I was his favorite child. But Helen got a severe scolding. I was not allowed to drive again until after I was twelve years old, but I did anyway. After watching me drive underage for years, the town patrolman said he would have to take action. Instead of a ticket, he gave me a driver's license.

During the summertime, one chore never ended: killing flies on the big front porch lined with rockers! The big front porch was where the family gathered to shell peas and beans, to knit and crochet, for my father to read his three daily newspapers, to discuss the weather, to crack and shell pecans, and to make any necessary plans.

I hated the long, hot, summer months, the flies, the mosquitoes, and no air conditioning, but I loved having my relatives visit. My Grandmother Gray lived with us during the warm months. She and my aunts loved to sit on the front porch and rock in the big rocking chairs. When my aunts came to visit, needing a fourth to play bridge, they taught me how to play when I was ten. For my thirteenth birthday party, I had three tables of bridge and proceeded to teach my friends how to play.

When I was an 8th grader, I was tall and slender and having a fun time with my friends. My girlfriends and I would exchange weekends at each other's homes: Millie at Mackey Point, and Douglas in Grahamville. Douglas was a girl two years older than I with two brothers who had three male friends, one of whom was old enough to drive. The group of us picnicked, swam in the river, practiced ballroom dancing, and went to movies. In the wintertime, the group came to our house and I fixed them cocoa and toast. My only other cooking skills were making fudge and fixing salad. So much for my culinary artistry!

I was distraught in the 8th grade because after a long bout with pneumonia, the doctor said I was physically unable to play basketball, a sport I loved. But, I did play in the 9th grade and was captain of the team in the 10th grade. My height and long arms gave me an edge on jumping.

I had no transportation to town to practice basketball. I would ride the school bus home after school, saddle a horse, and ride back into town to practice. Friends of mine who lived on the other side of town did the same thing. Often, we would boldly ride our horses to meet at the drugstore for a Coke or ice cream. During those days, the drugstore offered curb service, even on horseback.

I loved school and was a top student who seldom had to bring a book home to study. I could always do several things at one time. My homework was always done for one class during another class because I hated taking those heavy books home.

All my siblings studied long and hard to make passing grades. I was an avid reader and read every book in the house from *Animal Husbandry* to *The Last of the Mohicans*. What an education for this young lass!

I was influenced by my Uncle Lincoln to excel in Latin and math, and I did. In school, there was a boy who was a tad smarter than I. In the 9ᵗʰ grade, we both won the competitions for being the best in the county in Latin and math. We went to Columbia, the capital of South Carolina, to compete for being the best in the state. *We were defeated!* It seemed that the little, small-town schools were not as advanced as the large city schools.

When I was in high school, most of my friends took home economics, learning to sew and cook. Not me. I took Latin, higher math, business, accounting, typing, and shorthand. I was also president of the Commercial Club.

For me, high school was a time for learning and having fun. It ended with an experience that no one, including me, ever expected!

Now, I have even more tales to tell…

Graveyard Island

My Uncle Jessie and Aunt Bea owned a small island called Graveyard Island less than an hour from our house in the Low Country of South Carolina. It was on the saltwater Chechessee River. On the island is a small Civil War cemetery where former slaves were buried. At nighttime, you could see the lights of the famous marine base, Parris Island, on your left, and Hilton Head on your right.

My uncle built a two-bedroom cottage with a huge screened-in porch. When all the army cots were unfolded, it would sleep many people. In the summer, on Wednesday afternoons, when the stores and businesses closed, our family often went to Graveyard Island. Occasionally, we would spend the night sleeping on the screened-in porch.

You could swim, fish, shrimp, or crab. A big, iron, black pot was used to cook the crabs. A hunk of bacon added to the pot gave the crabs that special Low Country flavor. The fish were cooked in a deep frying pan, and another large pot was used to cook the shrimp. The tablecloth was many layers of newspaper. You had to peel your own shrimp and pick out your own crabmeat, making sure that you discarded the dead man's fingers and other inedibles. When there was no catch, we ate peanut butter and jelly sandwiches.

One night, when our parents were not spending the night and the men had gone mullet fishing, we persuaded our young Aunt Bea to take us skinny-dipping. Covered with large towels, down to the edge of the river we went. The tide was high and the moonlight was glistening on the water.

We were unaccustomed to not being protected by swimsuits. The swirl of the water felt strange on our nude bodies. Suddenly, one cousin screamed, "Something touched me!"

"Me too!" said another one.

I was already on my way to shore, followed closely by the whole group. Grabbing our towels without catching our breath, we all, including Aunt Bea, ran to the cottage.

After a quick shower, hair toweled almost dry, in pajamas, we began to discuss the commotion in the water. A shark, a jellyfish, or a crab was suggested. "Perhaps a real mermaid," said I, who had not been touched.

Nighttime was always fun time for us children. Our imaginations would come alive as we gazed through the long moss swaying in the breeze toward the graveyard. Hovering around the graves, we would see white things that seemed to come closer and closer to us. Shivering, we dared each other to go to the graveyard to see the ghosts. Sometimes, we all held hands and stepped outside so we could see them better. As they seemed to get closer, we scurried back inside. We would hide our heads under our pillows, scarcely daring to breathe. Aunt Bea would come out to investigate the silence. We would sit up when she spoke to us, but the ghosts would have disappeared.

We were never able to show her those elusive, eerie, white creatures!

Billy

I never had any riding lessons—just got on a horse and held on. But riding did come naturally. I remember one horse my father bought named Billy, a spectacular white horse with a *mean-n-n-n* streak.

The top of the dam beside the duck pond was my favorite place to ride. Riding along the dam, Billy would go between two trees and try to squeeze my legs off. I would have to lift my legs into the saddle to keep them from being maimed. When that ruse didn't work, he would start for home, and could he run! Nothing could hold him back. I would just hold on! I have to admit I was scared and would be a little shaky by the time he would come to a halt at the barn.

Even though he was not trustworthy, would not let another horse get ahead of him, and no one else would ride him, I begged my father to keep Billy for me to ride. I loved showing off his fancy steps as he pranced down the street. People would come out of their shops and homes to see him.

No wonder the town folks liked to watch Billy—Billy used to perform in the circus!

The Torn Screen

My older sister, Helen, started smoking while in high school. She tore about a ten-inch hole in the lower screen of the window behind her bed in order to throw her cigarette out whenever she heard my parents coming. She went off to college when I was about twelve years old and I began sleeping in her twin bed by the window.

Late one hot, summer evening, since we didn't have air conditioning back then, I had the window open and was reading in bed. I heard a kinda rustle outside and turned my head just in time to see the finger of a black hand slowly coming through the screen of the window. I was too frightened to scream. The finger continued to slowly creep through the screen. When the hand came through and that finger touched me on the shoulder, the screams began, waking up the entire household.

My father and brother, Vernon, ran into my room to see what kind of problem could cause such horrible sounds. They immediately recognized the hand as belonging to Charley, one of my father's black employees, who was so frightened by my screams that he was almost white-faced. He thought he was touching the shoulder of my brother, Vernon. He had run out of gas while driving one of my father's trucks from work and wanted Vernon to refuel the empty tank. You see, my father kept a regular gas tank in the back yard for use in his road building, farm equipment, and our cars.

Needless to say, Charley never used this method of getting gas again!

Under Lock and Key

Although she was older than I, I had a friend who was in my church activities, Girl Scouts, and on the basketball team with me. After some of these activities, she would invite several of us over to her house. Her mother, though in ill health, was always gracious. We enjoyed the expensive games and library filled with encyclopedias and books for all ages. I remember the huge dictionary on a lectern.

After her mother's health declined and she could no longer live at home, my friend's busy attorney/father hired a sorta governess/housekeeper. This lady would not allow us to come inside the house or allow the games outside the house.

On the second floor was a storage pantry that this lady kept under lock and key. My friend knew where the key was kept, so she would open the window and throw out candy, cookies, nuts, or fruit for us to catch. Then, she would join us outside to eat the treats. This self-confident, self-reliant young lady was determined her friends would have the refreshments she was accustomed to serving.

No lock or key could stop her!

The Housekeeper's Night Off

Johnny Jr., was the four-year-old son of my favorite Aunt Gladys. She and her attorney/politician husband lived in Columbia, South Carolina. They had a live-in housekeeper who had a 7th grade grandson, Edward, who came each day to play with and entertain their son. Occasionally, Edward spent the night.

Having three smaller brothers made me a prime candidate to be their guest for two weeks each summer. Being a little country girl, I enjoyed the capital city, the big stores, and other interesting places.

My aunt's best friend had five children. The oldest was a sixteen-year-old boy named Wallace. Wallace and his siblings included me in their summer activities and outings. It just so happened that on the housekeeper's night off, Wallace's parents and my uncle and aunt were invited to a special dinner on a houseboat at the lake. Wallace offered to stay with Johnny Jr., Edward, and me until they would return at around nine o'clock. The housekeeper prepared a picnic for us before she left.

Wallace and I joined Johnny Jr. and Edward in their outdoor games, then, brought our picnic outside. Afterwards, we all went for a long walk until it began to get dark. Edward took Johnny Jr. for his bath and jammies. After one of his board games, Johnny Jr. was ready for bed. Before Edward could finish reading him a story, he was asleep. Edward brought a quilt and laid on the floor of the den, and before Wallace and I had finished our card game, he too was asleep.

It was now after nine o'clock with no sign of the adults. I was interested in hearing about Wallace's city school and activities, so time passed quickly. The only thing I remembered of the conversation was when Wallace asked me if I knew how to poach eggs. I told him I didn't even know how to boil them! He said he couldn't marry me then. His favorite course in school was gourmet cooking.

The clock struck twelve. I thought it was time to start worrying about the adults. We checked the phone; it was working fine. The frantic parents came in after one o'clock and found a peaceful house with all occupants fast asleep. There had been an electrical storm at the lake and they couldn't get the houseboat to the dock.

Without knowing it, thirteen-year-old Carolyne, had just had her first date!

The CCC

In the early thirties, many young men enlisted in a branch of service called the Civilian Conservation Corps, known as the CCC. The government rented our farm as one location for their large training camp. They set up temporary barracks and taught the enlistees about crops and all phases of farming. Many of these young men had never seen a cow milked or land plowed. The unmarried girls of Ridgeland were so excited about all the available young guys. I was just fourteen and already infatuated with a school friend.

Although I could have had the inside edge, I was not interested!

The First Time I Lied

In my first year of high school, there were a number of new boys from other schools that I did not know in elementary school. I noticed one of them watching me, just happening to be going up the stairs at the same time I was, and arranging to sit behind me in study hall. He was a dark-haired, dark-eyed, flirty, brash type of guy. I really wasn't interested in him. Besides, I wasn't allowed to single date. I was busy group dating, playing basketball, making great grades, riding horseback, driving a car, and enjoying my girlfriends. Life was my bowl of cherries.

He was three years older than I and two grades above me. He loved and excelled in softball and boxing. How he managed to get into my study hall and sit behind me, I never found out. It seemed that everywhere I turned, he was there. With his persistence and romantic notes, he broke down my resistance. He would get another couple to go to the movies with us or we could go to church. Pretty soon, he was dropping by asking my parents if I could ride to town with him to get a Coke. He was quite conniving.

Soon, he was coming over on Friday nights, bringing me a box of chocolate-covered Brazil nuts. He and my father liked chocolate-covered Brazil nuts. Next, he began to help my father finish his game of solitaire so that my father would go to bed. Oops, another game was dealt. He'd really have to hurry it along because bedtime was called at ten o'clock.

On my birthday of the next year, the young man gave me a small diamond. My parents were not happy about this. Of course, I fully intended to finish school before marriage. By now, I was truly infatuated with this Romeo. I fell in love for the first time even though I missed the camaraderie of the boy-girl group I formerly ran around with.

My Aunt Clifton Carolyn, who lived in Washington, D.C., came to visit us one summer and my future was plotted. She and my Uncle Jimmy wanted me to come to Washington to make my debut into society at their expense. She spoke of the handsome naval officers, the beautiful clothes, the protocol. This gangly little country girl was petrified!

I, who wore my brother's pants and shirt, I, whose idea of dressing up was a quick shower and shampoo, a fresh blouse and skirt, and a dab of lipstick. The very thought of leaving my high school sweetheart was devastating.

One cold January day, I told my parents I had been invited to spend the weekend with my good friend, Millie, and that the young man was going to pick me up around nine o'clock Saturday morning to take me there. I put on my new Christmas dress, it was gray with a red velvet collar and a matching red velvet tam, then stuffed the overnight bag until it was bulging. My parents suspected nothing because I had never lied before. I am so sorry that I did.

Shortly before it was time to leave for the lovely Washington trip, there was an elopement in the family.

Chapter 4
Life of Adjustments

The Days of Trial and Error

MARRIED life was quite an adjustment for this young girl, avid for learning, no school, no money, almost completely isolated from friends and family.

We finally managed to rent two rooms near the lumber mill where my husband, Ray, worked. With our own bedroom furniture, a radio, a borrowed kerosene stove, a homemade table, two donated folding chairs, and numerous pasteboard boxes, we began housekeeping.

I had learned to cook vegetables, grits, rice, and other plain foods from my mother-in-law. Everyday, I tried to make biscuits the way I had seen my mother-in-law make hers. Everyday, we'd throw them away. One day, Ray even tried to use one for a baseball. Then, after several weeks, I discovered the oven of the kerosene stove was the problem, not me. After many painful attempts, my cooking became quite tasteful.

During the first years of our marriage, my mother would come to eat lunch with us almost once a week. She would bring us shelled pecans that she spent hours picking up from under the pecan trees and shelling; fringed, soft dish towels that she made from feed sacks; cane syrup; blackberry jelly; butter, cream, milk, eggs; bacon and pork; and fresh vegetables from her garden. My in-laws shared their chickens and eggs. Otherwise, we'd have gone hungry. During the Depression years, all these things made a big difference in our lives.

I also tried my hand at learning to sew a little. I never really enjoyed it, but it surely helped out on housedresses. Learning to iron was also an experience. I had to heat several irons on top of the wood stove. Each was made of real iron. Most everything was starched: shirts, dresses, and pillowcases. These had to be sprinkled down first, and then ironed. It was very easy to scorch them, which I often did.

By now, we were to move into a house with three bedrooms, a bath, dining room, living room, breakfast room, pantry, many closets, and two screen porches. Our rent was about six dollars a month.

On the day we were to move, my brother Vernon, age twenty-one, was killed in an accident. Our clothes were packed. I was very upset over his death, and not being able to find my shoes added to my further frustrations.

Vernon's insurance was divided among us. We were able to buy our first car, a Jenny Lind bed for the second bedroom, and a dependable clock.

Ray's father had taught him the lumber business. He was good not only at selling lumber, but also at making things from the wood. He made us a porch swing and lawn furniture as well as a cedar chest. They were nice looking too.

We and the other young people of the neighborhood particularly enjoyed playing Ping-Pong in our dining room. We also enjoyed playing card games such as Flinch and Setback. I played bridge with female friends also.

Later, the company for whom Ray worked built us a house across the street. Money was still not plentiful. I ordered small plants at little cost, got cuttings from my mother, and fertilized and nurtured them. We sprigged the lawn with centipede grass that other people were throwing away. It wasn't long until we had the prettiest yard in the neighborhood.

I began to be very active in church and community affairs. My days and nights were busy, busy, busy.

But still, I have tales to tell...

The Lost Pair

After I married, one of my girlfriends, Jennie, and I went to Savannah to see the movie *Wuthering Heights*. I was so interested in it that I relaxed and took off my shoes. People entering our row of seats kicked my shoes forward, as did the others in the rows in front of us. They had been kicked so far, that in the dark, I could no longer see them.

As Catherine called, "Heeaath–cliff, Heeaath–cliff," instead of crying with the rest of the audience, we held tissues over our mouths to keep from laughing about my dilemma.

When the movie ended, my shoes were nowhere in sight. We searched and searched and on the front row, we finally found two shoes waiting to be slipped on my stocking-covered feet. The laughter started again.

This time we didn't have to cover our mouths so no one would hear us. The theater was already empty.

An Unusual Church Service

When I was young, black and white people attended different churches. There was a famous black bishop whose car had a replica of an angel on top of it. He sometimes preached near where I lived at a church that was attended by black people. We wondered what this famous bishop was like, so a group of us decided to visit the church when he was to preach.

Near dusk, we entered the church already full of people

and seated ourselves on the back pew. We were told, "Follow me. We have another place for you to sit." Not knowing what to expect, we were taken to seats near the pulpit.

When hymns were played, worshippers raised their arms in praise and moved rhythmically in the aisles. Their shouts and chants rang out as the spirit moved them. Some even lost consciousness. Our church was so different from this church that we felt uncomfortable. When we tried to leave, we were told, "The worship service isn't over yet." We resumed our seats.

The time came for the passing of the offering plates. None of us females had brought a purse or money. While a hymn was played, the males in our group reached in their pockets and placed their coins in the plate. When the plates were taken to the bishop, he looked accusingly at us and said, "Some of you are not giving God His share!"

Another hymn was played and the offering plates were passed again. The males opened their wallets and placed a dollar bill in the offering plate. This was during the height of the Depression! The preacher looked at the money in the plates and looked directly at us again with his strange, piercing eyes. This time he said, "Some people are cheating God!"

The offering plates were passed a third time. Each male placed a five dollar bill in the plate. The five dollars was our rent money for an entire month!

After sitting for two hours and listening to a fiery sermon, the preacher ended the service with a loud, "Amen," echoed by most of the congregation. We weren't among the ones waiting to shake the bishop's hand, but we were among the ones who quickly made their way to their cars.

We no longer wondered what the bishop was like. Now we knew!

The Looming Bridges

I was in a dilemma. A dearly loved relative was inebriated and planned to drive the five hours home. My only solution, since I couldn't persuade him to stay overnight, was for me to drive him home. Now, I had no experience driving long distances.

In the beginning, all went well, for he was soon snoring. As we approached Charleston, there loomed the high Cooper River Bridge with its many curves. I remember the first time I crossed it. I was not driving, so I dared to look down at the river—once, once only. It was like being at the top of the Empire State Building and descending on a roller coaster. But this time, I was driving and my inebriated passenger awoke and did not appreciate my cautious driving. He put his heavy foot on top of my summer sandal and pressed and pressed. I was now speeding beyond the limit, and worse, I could not remove his foot. I was terrified!

Never had I prayed more fervently. Finally, during a few seconds of straightaway, telling him he was hurting my foot, I was able to push his leg away, taking his foot off the pedal. Soon he was fast asleep again. Slowly and cautiously, I exited the rest of the bridge easily. My sleeping passenger did not awaken again until he reached home.

After we passed through Charleston, the Ashley River Bridge loomed ahead, but its height did not faze me. God had heard my prayers and already answered them!

Changes

At the beginning of World War II, our first child, Diane, was born. Three years later, our only son, Steve, was born. When Steve was five years old, our second daughter, Terry, was born. Several years earlier, we had picket-fenced the yard. With a sandbox, portable pool, swing set, and slide, our children stayed outdoors in our yard most of the time. So did the rest of the nearby children. I practically babysat the whole neighborhood.

Meanwhile, Ray was exempt from military service because lumber was essential to the war effort. His sales territory was expanded. The company wished us to move to a more central location. Atlanta was finally chosen.

This Country Girl was about to move to the big city!

Part Two

Life in Atlanta – Southern Lady

*Carolyne, the country girl,
who becomes a Southern lady.*

The Big City

UNLESS you have...

— admired the dogwoods, magnolias, daffodils, and azaleas that adorn Atlanta in the springtime;
— appreciated the red, yellow, orange, and golden leaves of trees that showcase the city in the fall;
— learned to say "y'all" with two syllables;
— learned that brunch can mean either breakfast or lunch; dinner can mean either lunch or supper;
— eaten grits, bacon, eggs, and toast for breakfast;
— enjoyed a backyard barbecue of grilled chicken, pork, steak, hamburgers, or hot dogs, with or without barbecue sauce;
— eaten fried chicken, rice and gravy, butter beans, biscuits, homemade banana pudding, and sweet tea for Sunday lunch, and eaten the leftovers for supper;
— listened for the melodic sound of the ice cream truck approaching your street;
— taken your children to the library every Saturday morning;
— rummaged through neighborhood yard sales for treasures;
— attended street festivals, arts and crafts sales, and local concerts;
— watched kudzu grow six feet overnight taking over entire roadsides;
— driven beside bicycles, joggers, skateboards, and baby strollers on a sunny day;
— watched the entire city of Atlanta shut down after a prediction of two inches of snow that often never came;
— stood in line at the grocery store buying extra food just in case the snow did come;
— sat in morning, noon, and afternoon traffic jams;
— given directions using landmarks like The Big Chicken and Spaghetti Junction;

— wondered how Atlanta was built over Underground Atlanta;

— figured out the difference in downtown and uptown Atlanta;

— explored Fernbank Forest and perched on elephant rock;

— visited the Fernbank Museum of Natural History and enjoyed a film at the IMAX Theater;

— attended a touring Broadway play at Atlanta's famous Fox Theater with its Moorish architecture and twinkling stars scattered among moving clouds on the ceiling;

— visited the home of Margaret Mitchell where she wrote *Gone With the Wind* and the home of Joel Chandler Harris, famous for his *Uncle Remus* tales;

— climbed Stone Mountain and tried to spot your home in the distance;

— seen the Cyclorama with its reenactment of the Civil War;

— survived driving a carload of kids to Six Flags Over Georgia;

...then you've never enjoyed real Southern living in the big city of Atlanta, Georgia!

Chapter 5
Life With My Family

Dreams and Screams

WE packed, said goodbye to loved ones, and left the Low Country for the big city of Atlanta. After living in the Atlanta area for three years, we invested in a much-needed larger home in the old historic district of Druid Hills. The house was once one of the Druid Hills showcases. The property backed up to Fernbank Forest. The virgin trees, fauna, creeks, and caves were an explorer's delight for the children. We didn't see them except at mealtime. They loved it!

These homes were built for maids, butlers, and a yardman, which we could not afford. So, three years later, we built my dream house nearby, which required very little care and had many rooms and closets. But, the house I loved didn't bring love and happiness. There were many ups and downs.

I began having a frightening, reoccurring dream that continued for years. Each dream was different, but always the same. Someone was chasing me and I was running—not only to escape from the person chasing me, but also to keep from being killed. There always seemed to be hills and steps and places too steep for me to climb. My family was awakened night after night with my pitiful cries, "*Hee-e-lp* me! Please *help* me!" Just as the assailant was about to catch me, these cries and the family waking me kept me from being killed!

A year after we moved into the dream house, I enrolled in business school, taking a two-year course in one. I started to work in a one-girl office across town. Later, I lived in other houses and had other jobs, which led to my working as a corporate accountant in the mortgage industry for almost 30 years before I retired.

But first, I have even more tales to tell…

Who's Who?

We had come from South Carolina to Atlanta to close the loan on our very first home. Several weeks before, we had spent days looking at houses. We finally found one in our price range that embraced us and was near an elementary school. Perhaps it was the large oak in the backyard with a limb just right for a rope swing for the children that really sold us on this house.

Sitting in an attorney's office with the friendly real estate agent along with the nice couple whose house we were buying, we signed mountains of papers. The attorney handed us our stack that declared us the new owners with occupancy on the Fourth of July. What a happy day—moving to Atlanta into our very own house!

There was an apprehensive moment as another attorney entered the room. Something was wrong with my signature. They began questioning me at length. Was I the infamous Carolyne T. Wynne wanted for questioning by the IRS and the FBI?

I finally convinced them that I was a small-town country girl from South Carolina. Again, they placed the "very dear to us" papers in our hands. Our special day had not been darkened. We went on to dinner at Mammy's Shanty to celebrate and make moving plans.

For years, I received many calls intended for the other Carolyne T. Wynne. From the nature of the calls and the many invitations to go partying, I decided she must have been a very popular lady.

When I finally stopped receiving the strange, intriguing calls, an unusual thing happened. I went to my hairdresser who said she had expected me two days earlier according to her appointment book. A stranger had arrived saying she was Carolyne T. Wynne.

I told the hairdresser my story. The only thing my hairdresser remembered about her was that she was very attractive. She hasn't returned. Was the mysterious stranger the infamous Carolyne T. Wynne?

Even my hairdresser doesn't know for sure!

Peaches

When my children were young, they loved to hear stories about my early life as well as many tales that I read or made up. A special story that Terry particularly liked came from the novel *Michael O'Halloran* by Gene Stratton–Porter. I don't remember much of it.

Michael was about eleven years old when his mother died. He took care of himself selling newspapers on the New York streets. He was able to avoid being sent to an orphanage by many shrewd maneuvers. Of course, the authorities never knew he was living alone in a tiny apartment that had formerly been occupied by both him and his mother.

Michael used a little wagon to haul his newspapers around. He also had regular customers to whom he delivered the newspapers. One day, as he delivered a paper to an apartment, he heard a little whimpering sound. At first, he thought maybe it was a cat. Then, as he continued to listen, he thought maybe it was even a baby. As the sound continued, he knocked softly on the door. Hearing no answer, he slowly opened the door. All that he could see was a pile of old newspapers and rags in a corner. Then, he realized that was where the sound was coming from. When he went closer, he discovered the sound was from a little girl about six years old, although she only looked about four.

He finally understood that her grandfather, her only living relative, had died and the furniture had been sold to pay for his funeral. Her parents had died a year ago. The authorities were coming to take the little girl to the orphanage that very day. Now, an orphanage back then was thought of as a terrible place, more like a prison.

Michael saw that the little girl was crippled and unable to walk. He placed some rags in his nearby empty wagon and quickly placed her in it. Next, he covered her up with some more rags and put papers on top of them. Carefully looking around, he maneuvered them to an alley just as he saw an official car parking in front of the building. The authorities had come for her. He continued down several alleys until he came to his building. Furtively, he carried her up the stairs and quickly unlocked his door.

She was so dirty, he just placed her back on the floor. He put water on to heat, brought out his small washtub, and while the water was heating, put clean sheets on the bed. Searching in the bottom drawer of the chest, he found one of his mother's soft nightgowns.

He filled the tub with warm water, found a big bar of soap, and a clean washcloth and towel. As he started to pick up the little girl to put her in the tub, she began to cry. She didn't want to get in the tub. Then, Michael told her he would put her in the wagon, take her back to her room, and she would have to go to the orphanage.

She finally quieted down and he separated her from the filthy rags and paper, and placed her in the warm water. She relaxed and began to like it. Then, he generously soaped the washcloth and started on her face, neck, arms, and then her hair. It took several soapings and more warm water before she was clean.

And when the bath was finished, her hair toweled dry, and she was in a clean gown, Michael found his mother's hairbrush and began on the tangled hair. She didn't like that, but tolerated it. When he had finished, he found one of his mother's ribbons and tied it around her hair. Her hair almost hung down to her little waist.

Finally, he took a good look at her. He looked at her face, so fair and unblemished, cheeks with a hint of color, and the soft, golden hair that was now beginning to curl. As Michael handed her his mother's mirror and she saw herself, she began to smile and then to laugh!

Michael, too, started to laugh and said, "Why you look like you have a peaches and cream complexion. I'm just going to call you *Peaches!*"

A Lovely World

When our children were young, each summer and fall we would vacation in Gatlinburg, Tennessee, for a weekend. The children loved hiking on the nature trails best. The most exhilarating part of hiking was to reach a stream of rushing water with rugged rocks.

In the summer, we would take off our shoes, find a smooth rock, and dangle our hot, dusty feet in the cold, swirling water. Sometimes, I thought that I saw Indians darting from bush to bush and wondered if these were the very stones they had used to cross this stream.

In the fall, after an early frost, the scattered leaves that had fallen were red and gold. It seemed so easy to breathe—no smoke or fumes or gas—the air was so fresh. The silence, the birds, and the wind made their own music, a song without a tune. I thought then, "All's right with the world; what a lovely world we live in."

While I sat there meditating, I sensed that God sat beside me, approving "His Workmanship."

Chapter 6
Life With My Friends

Laughter and Tears

THIS is a story about Marcia—a true story, a funny story, a strange story, a sad story! I'm sure there are adequate words to describe Marcia, but I don't know them. Perhaps these little incidents will help describe her.

I had gone to her house to pick her up for an early meeting. Going into the kitchen for a drink of water, I noticed the sink. "Oh, Marcia," I said. "Your beautiful sterling is in the dishwater with the iron frying pan and butcher knives."

"Don't let it bother you," she replied. "One of my little girls was so fretful last night, I just didn't get back to it. Besides, wedding presents should be used, not just looked at."

There was another incident at a luncheon for about forty women at the Piedmont Driving Club. Each lady was asked to introduce herself. These ladies took great pride in telling of their many accomplishments as they gave their names. It was getting far past the serving hour; our tummies were rumbling. It finally became my turn. I hastily stated, "I'm Carolyne Wynne, flunky to the vice president," and sat down. Two chairs down, Marcia simply said that she was flunky to the flunky and sat down. The message had been received with laughter. It was just a few minutes later that lunch was served.

On another occasion, we went shopping in downtown Atlanta. In those days, we wore our heels, white gloves, and little hats with veils. It was one of those times after lunch in the Magnolia Room at Rich's Department Store. Marcia's two-and-a-half-year-old, tired and sleepy, wanting to go home, had a good screaming, kicking, temper tantrum on the floor of the fine jewelry department.

Deciding to turn this into a humorous situation, I walked past her, stating loudly, "I wonder where the mother of this disturbing child could be?"

Marcia followed me quickly, stepped over her child, and replied, "I wish I knew, I would give her a piece of my mind." The little one, not getting any attention, picked herself up and ran to catch up with us.

Lastly, is a series of events I'll never forget. We had just moved into a brand-new house. Workmen were coming to finish up and several deliveries were to be made. It was on a Monday morning when Marcia, who was awaiting her third child, called, wanting us to get together for the day. I explained my dilemma and suggested that we do it the next day. Oh, how I regretted this decision!

We chatted a bit, then she said, "Carolyne, you'll never guess what I'm doing. I'm watching a rosebud unfold before my very eyes." Then hearing my commotion, she concluded, "We took the girls to their grandparents' yesterday, and the only thing I have left to do is to bring this baby into the world."

About five o'clock the next morning, the phone rang. A mutual friend of ours said, "I'm at Georgia Baptist Hospital, can you come?"

"Is it Marcia's baby?" I asked.

"The baby is fine. It's Marcia," she replied.

I was there in about thirty minutes, but that wasn't fast enough. The doctor was just entering the room. We didn't need to hear the words to know what he was about to say.

Marcia's husband gave me the keys to their home, asking me to answer the phone. Meanwhile, our friend went with him to the airport to meet Marcia's parents, who had been called earlier. I called a couple of our friends to meet me at Marcia's house.

We went into the bedroom to change the linens. There by the bed, was a newly decorated bassinet. For some reason, we pulled the coverlet back, and there were two slips of paper: one with a girl's name and one with a boy's name.

Marcia had named her newborn baby son!

A Squirming Success

A close friend of the family had a very cute, very headstrong, and very active son named Ricky. Before he could spell, Ricky's mother and I took him and my daughter Terry on a five-hour driving trip to the Blue Ridge Mountains. Ricky didn't want to go. To motivate him, I told Ricky that several places along the way had big mountain bears in cages by their stores.

After driving a few hours, I stopped the car and told Terry, who was older than Ricky, to go inside the store and ask if they had a "b-e-a-r," spelling each letter separately. Before Terry could open her door, four-year-old Ricky had jumped out of the car and had already asked if the store had a "b-e-a-r." This smart little boy knew that whatever a "b-e-a-r" was, he wanted to see it. Soon afterwards, we found out that Ricky had a very high IQ.

When he was in the 1st grade, Ricky was hard to discipline. His mother explained to the principal that Ricky had to know who was boss. The first day of school, Ricky was disruptive. The teacher sent him to the principal's office. "Ricky," the principal said, "When you misbehave in class, we use the 'board of education.' Do you know what that is?" Squirming in his seat, he shook his head. Pulling out a long, flat, wooden board, she said, "This is the 'board of education.'" The principal had made her point. Ricky returned to his classroom and never had to be sent to the principal's office again.

When Ricky visited my house for lunch, he wanted to fix his own sandwich. First, he spread mayonnaise on his bread. Then he sliced and added Vienna sausage followed by saltine crackers. His culinary abilities were quite unusual.

Once, his mother thought Ricky was lost. She and her friends searched for him for hours. Finally, he was found. He had been happily playing near the big pond in the huge old cemetery in back of their property.

Sometimes, Terry babysat for Ricky at our home. One day, Ricky enjoyed playing with her for a while, but then, he wanted to do something he shouldn't. When Terry told him, "No," he said he was going home and left. Up the street he walked. Terry followed him, trying to coax him to return. When he crossed the busy four-lane street of traffic, she gave up. She was not allowed to cross this dangerous street.

For a child who hated discipline and rules, what a surprise that as an adult, Ricky chose a twenty-two year career that included both. This adventuresome child became a United States naval chief petty officer serving his country on submarines, submarine rescue ships, and aircraft carriers throughout the world.

This retired chief petty officer still eats Vienna sausage and saltine cracker sandwiches.

Patsy

Patsy was an abandoned puppy, just a few days old. She was brought home by my daughter, Diane, from a football game. She was white with dark spots. Although she was not ugly, she could never have won a blue ribbon for beauty. Her legs were too short, her ears were too long, her eyes were too sad, and her bark was too loud. This smart little dog loved the outdoors. The sky was her friend.

One night, a mountain goat wandered into our yard. No one in our neighborhood slept much that night for Patsy's continual barking. The next morning, a neighbor called animal control to pick up a loud, vicious dog at our address. Patsy hurried to greet them. Licking their hands, she then lay on her back to have her tummy scratched.

Animal control left with the mountain goat!

Chapter 7
Life With My Mishaps

The Holiday With a Bang

IT was the Fourth of July. My family loved cooking outside on the barbecue grill. This particular grill was like a huge brick fireplace attached to the back of the carport. The chicken was marinating in the kitchen. The baked beans were seasoned and the corn on the cob was husked and ready for the grill. A crisp salad was chilling in the refrigerator. The rolls were sitting by the paper plates. The watermelon was waiting to be cut.

After I put charcoal lighter on the charcoals, I heard the phone ring. I went inside the house to answer it. The conversation lasted much longer than I expected. Saying goodbye, I picked up the long matches and went outside to light the grill.

I lit the match, stepped back, and threw it on the charcoal. Boom! An explosion! Things flew up and crashed down everywhere—bricks, grill, and charcoal! Single-handedly, I had blown up the barbecue grill.

I had invented a new form of fireworks to celebrate Independence Day!

Disaster Strikes

It was on a hot Friday night in July when we had a flash flood. The rain fell by buckets instead of by drops. My oldest daughter, Diane, called me at the hospital where I was on volunteer duty. She said that the six-inch babbling brook beside our home was over the patio and rising. "Get everything off of the floor and get the cars to the top of the hill, and I'll come right home," I said.

It took me 45 minutes instead of 10 to get home because of the downpour. Reaching my street, I left the car at the top of the hill along with others already parked there. I could see the water rushing across the street at the bottom of the hill where I lived. I, in my Red Cross uniform, white nurse's shoes, and umbrella, walked past two houses to get to my home.

Diane stood in nearly two feet of water under the carport. She had been home alone when the flood started. She explained it had taken her 20 minutes to find her pet cat before she could place him in her car and move it to the top of the hill. By then, it was too late to move Terry's Valiant or rescue anything from the house. Glancing to the side of the house, I saw the patio furniture floating down what was now a raging stream. I could only wave goodbye.

My youngest daughter, Terry, then arrived home by bus. Seeing me standing in the rain, holding my umbrella in disbelief, she greeted me with, "Hello, Mary Poppins."

Terry entered the house and the phone rang. The caller asked, "What are you doing?"

"I'm standing in my bedroom in three feet of water," Terry answered.

An electrician waded up and said he could turn off the electricity if I would show him the fuse box. On entering the living room, I saw the six-foot stereo floating in three feet of water. The short electrician climbed on the ironing board to reach the fuse box. The ironing board collapsed, he fell off, and I thought he had been electrocuted. Fortunately, he was only shocked.

Firemen came in and told us to get out and leave the doors open. When the water subsided, the open doors would help the water to get out too. Later, I found large burn spots on the hardwood floor caused from the electricity.

Outside, the rain had slacked up and we waded to higher ground. There we stood with no flood insurance, no dry clothes, and all we could think of was the disaster inside of the house. Our beautiful white sectional sofa, mattresses, clothing—everything ruined in a matter of hours. We would never be able to replace the cherished old photos.

In spite of the desolation I was feeling, I could not help but laugh when Terry called out, "Look Mom, there goes your wig floating down the creek!"

The Crash

While driving down a busy four-lane road with my daughter, Terry, the brakes gave out on my car. It began rolling downhill during rush hour traffic, gaining speed as we passed houses, churches, and a large university. We were nearing a five-way intersection. I had to do something to stop the car before the traffic light changed.

"What do I do?" I calmly asked. "I guess we'll have to pick a place to crash." Should I hit the ongoing traffic, the telephone pole, certainly not the nearby gas tanks?

"How about that brick wall by the gas station?" Terry calmly suggested.

So *crash* into the brick wall I did! All the bricks tumbled to the ground. We and the car were unharmed, but found ourselves with a circle of onlookers. The gas station owner was among them. Amazingly, he wanted that wall down anyway. He simply requested that I remove the bricks.

I contacted my insurance company, only to find out that

I had no insurance. Due to a mix-up, my insurance had been cancelled. I immediately corrected the mistake.

A taxi ride later, at work, a coworker said she needed the bricks to build a terrace. When she went to get them, the gas station owner gave her not only the bricks, but also concrete blocks for her terrace foundation and a lamppost to light it!

If my brakes ever fail again, I now know to simply pull the emergency brake. But then, if I had known more about the use of the emergency brake before the crash, there would have been no reinstated insurance, no brick wall removal for the gas station, and no lovely lighted terrace!

The Speeding Ticket

It was a holiday weekend and I was driving our family and my oldest daughter's boyfriend to Callaway Gardens. The patrol cars were out in full force. I had been watching them in the rearview mirror as they reversed directions to catch speeders.

To my surprise, the boyfriend announced that he and my daughter planned to be married. In a state of shock, I forgot about the patrolmen. Then, I heard the siren.

I quickly pulled over and began to look for my driver's license. The nice-looking young patrolman said, "Ma'am, did you know you were driving 70 miles per hour in a 55 miles per hour zone?"

To my chagrin, my husband responded, "No sir, she was driving 85 miles per hour!"

"You have an option," the patrolman explained, handing me a ticket. "You can come with me right now to pay your fine, or you can spend the weekend in jail. By the way, if you pay the ticket now, you must pay in cash."

Away we went. Arriving at our destination to pay the fine, I joked in a friendly tone to the presiding officer, "What is your jail serving for lunch today?" After describing a delicious meal, I asked if all of us could stay for lunch in jail.

"No," he replied without a smile, "if you don't pay the fine, only you can stay." He told me the amount I owed.

The young officer who had issued the ticket said, "If she were my wife, I would charge her twice that amount."

After paying the fine, I held the door open for my family and me to quickly exit. I turned around and in my sweetest voice said to the young officer, "My sympathy to your wife."

A Rude Awakening

For the first time in my life, I was living in an apartment. Unfortunately, apartment living was not for me. I decided to buy another house. After some weeks, I found some townhouses that were in the right price range with the right interest rate.

Now, I've always loved a bargain. Despite the fact that my daughter, Terry, warned, "Mom, you know you're not going to like climbing stairs," I didn't listen.

My cohorts in mortgage decided they'd take a look at the townhouse. "Carolyne, you are just buying price and interest rates, but not quality," they told me. But, I didn't care to hear these things and decided to buy anyway.

I had not yet closed the loan, but was allowed to move in several days early. The day we moved, my daughter, Terry, and I only unpacked linens for our beds. Then, we put a few items in the refrigerator, and went out to eat.

Sometime after midnight, I was sound asleep when my bed began to shake violently. I woke up, startled. What was happening? Was it an earthquake? It couldn't be my imagination! Kinda holding on to things while wall-walking, I went into Terry's room. She was sitting up in bed. As we looked at each other in shock, we heard a train whistle and felt the rumble of *many* freight cars passing by. I had seen the train tracks directly across the street, but had no idea that passing trains would be like this!

"Oh my word! Will it be like this every night? What are we

going to do?" I asked.

"Oh, Mom, it's just a train. You could make friends with it and give it a name. How about Tallulah?" Then Terry, who planned to move out shortly anyway, began to laugh.

I, however, did not. The next morning, I was released from my contract and moved out within the week.

To this day, whenever we see or hear trains, we say, "There goes Tallulah!" Now, I too can laugh!

Chapter 8
Life On My Own

Yesterday's Answer to Today's Problems

I have two daughters who have difficulty with cooking. I have had them call me for a recipe on how to boil water. With many years of experience, I have a recipe that saves them time and money. "Girls," I say, "fill your cup with water and put it in the microwave for two minutes."

When I was a child, my mother would go to the garden early in the morning, pick beans, sit on the porch in a rocker, shell them, make fire in the wood stove, cook the beans with a streak of lean, and they would be ready for the noon meal. "Girls," I say, "just go to the frozen food section of the store, pick up a bag of beans, and put it in the microwave for five minutes."

The girls have a problem with sewing. "How do you make buttonholes?" they ask.

With much experience, I recommend, "Buy Velcro at the fabric store; then, you can do it in seconds."

And on the matter of disciplining children, never spank them or you'll be jailed for child abuse. Just give them lots of

hugs and when they are twenty-one, they'll hug you back.
Isn't experience a wonderful thing?

The Rocking Chair

Not long after my husband died, my daughter Diane, my
small grandchild, and I were watching television in the living
room. Now, when my grandchild was born, we had moved the
high-back Boston rocker from the bedroom to the living room
so we could rock the new baby the same way we had rocked
Terry years before.

Our eyes were drawn from the television to the rocker because it began slo-o-w-ly rocking, but no one was sitting in it.
As we began to wonder, the chair began to move a little faster,
then faster and faster. Our eyes were glued to the rocker as
it began rapidly rocking. We looked at each other—even the
two-year-old stopped playing with her toys to watch the rocker.
Could the dishwasher, washing machine, or an outside lawn
mower have caused the vibrations? None were in use.

"Dad, is that you?" I asked. There was a change in the
movement. The chair slo-o-w-ly stopped rocking.

Perhaps in his own way, Dad was answering my question.

Creatively Coping With Retirement

Two weeks after retirement, my home was organized and
spotless. There was no problem solving or deadlines. I was
bored! I found directions for making terrariums and made one
for my daughter, Terry, and one for me. Terry placed hers on
her desk at work in a large public area. Within two months, I
had more than forty requests for terrariums for Mother's Day.
Making them required many nature walks collecting moss, unusual pebbles, roots, and other crud. Each one was a different creation complete with miniature figurines such as turtles,
squirrels, rabbits, mushrooms, and owls.

Cold weather arrived and five hand-crocheted Afghans made their way to relatives for Christmas gifts. Next, there was a class in Greek, extensive travel, and volunteer work. My volunteer work included becoming one of the original ambassadors for the DeKalb County Convention & Visitors Bureau, treasurer of my homeowner's association, and treasurer of Life Enrichment Services, an organization for seniors.

Through Life Enrichment Services, many opportunities were presented. For the first time, I tried oil and acrylic painting, watercolors, and calligraphy; studied about Indians and archeology; expanded my knowledge of cryptology and investing; and became more aware of the world through interesting speakers.

I had to begin multitasking to finish my crafts and still have time to attend classes, play bridge twice a week, and do volunteer work three times a week. I would watch television, hold a conversation, and crochet, all at the same time. It took a year to finish the hand-crocheted bedspread and pillow shams for Terry's queen-size bed. There was also the cross-stitching of angels, orientals, bookmarks, and children from around the world. This didn't cost much money, but it did cost me a carpal tunnel surgery on each wrist.

Needless to say, I was no longer bored!

The Spider

They have been magnified and made into poetry. Perhaps some of the great architects of the day have copied their blueprints. Now, I have examined some of their homes very carefully and I cannot find the front door to the web. When the spider invited the fly into the parlor, how did the fly find the front door?

Spiders need never fear my daughter, Terry, invading their home for she is deathly afraid of them. Whenever she finds a spider or its web, she calls a relative, friend, or neighbor. To keep her from calling 9-1-1, I presented her with a can of spider killer.

The moral of this story is, "Don't invade my home and I won't destroy yours."

The Confession

Not long ago, I heard my daughter Terry say, "I cheated in my high school biology class, and with my mother's consent."

For this particular quarter, the project assignment was to collect a number of insects, an impossible task for someone who turned pale and shook all over at the sight of a small spider. Terry had a terrible fear of insects. Living alone, I have known her to call someone to come and kill an itsy-bitsy insect or some other creepy-crawly creature. Of course, she always declared that they were over six inches long.

Her brother, Steve, was quite the opposite. He had an elaborate insect collection of small, large, and unusual bugs he had caught himself. He had painted cigar boxes, cut Styrofoam to fit in them, and spaced and labeled each bug inside the box. Except for Terry, the rest of the family "oohed" and "aahed" each time Steve found a new, rare, or strange bug to add to his insect collection.

With the mother's approval, it was this collection that was turned in by Terry for her insect project. In the classroom, the teacher invited the other students to view this exotic collection. Terry received an A+.

I have felt the need for confession and forgiveness for years. When Terry's teacher retired and became a bridge partner, I had the opportunity. Her former students invited some of her friends, including me, to a dinner to honor her. After dinner, we were to read aloud special memories we had written about her and then give her our writings. I read my confession about the insect project. I expected forgiveness after asking for it. Instead, the teacher simply smiled and mouthed the words,

"Thank you."

At bridge the following week, she told me the room was so noisy, she couldn't hear a word I had said, but she did read my confession later. "Of course, I forgive you," she said.

Several weeks later, she was late for bridge and with a smile, she asked, "Now, will you forgive me?"

Laughingly, I did!

Vacations Then and Now

It wasn't easy to be a good mother, especially during vacation. When the time came to make a family decision on where to go on vacation, I was always outvoted four to one. Each year, they would make the same choice: the beach, the beach, let's go to Daytona Beach!

Each year, the same routine would develop. As soon as breakfast was finished, into swimsuits and down to conquer the crashing waves, low tide or high tide. Hunger pangs would signal lunchtime. How could little people eat so much? Before I could finish the first round of peanut butter and jelly sandwiches, they would be ready for seconds.

Time to rinse and hang out the swimsuits and sweep out the sand. Now, I would think, I can relax and work the daily crossword puzzle. By that time, the children had tired of their games and felt the call of the waves—just a cookie or two before they left.

As soon as the sun began to lower, it was expedient that we hurry to get some fresh seafood for supper before they starved to death. But, not before the wet towels were gathered, swimsuits rinsed and hung out, and the sand swept out again.

It was peaceful riding on the beach to the lighthouse, then strolling on the hard-packed sand at twilight. Surely, now I could work that crossword puzzle. That, too, was not to be —the children must go into the pool at night! After they were settled into their pajamas, there were more hunger pangs, and swimsuits to rinse, and more sand to sweep.

This was the routine we followed on vacation from pre-school to elementary school to high school and even to college. Each year as I was outvoted, I would tell myself to hang in there, your time will come.

As I live alone now, each year I vote for snow-covered mountains, plains, prairies, or other exotic places. Now, I have visited many states and almost a hundred countries. At the beginning of each adventure, I smile as I remember the hungry mouths, the sand, the wet towels, and the swimsuits.

But most of all, I remember the happy, smiling faces!

Return To My Childhood Home

My heart began to beat a little faster, like a child visiting the circus for the first time. My eyes were racing ahead of the car in which I was riding. I was going to see my childhood home that was sold after my father's death. I hadn't seen it in many years.

My mind began to remember: the row of pink crepe myrtles leading from the main road to the house; the high fence that the pink Dorothy Perkins roses climbed, providing flowers for proms and weddings during the spring and summer; the many beds of old-fashioned flowers—phlox, marigolds, pinks, zinnias, and cosmos—all the colors of the rainbow; the wide-spread lawn neatly trimmed; the huge low-limbed moss-covered oaks, so good for climbing and hanging swings; pine cones from the tall pines that wisteria climbed to the very top; the big old-fashioned porch with its many large rocking chairs—I could just see my mother and grandmother there snapping green beans, shelling butter beans, or cracking pecans.

I opened my eyes when my brother announced that we had arrived. Was he sure this was the right house?

There was no lawn, just a few clods of grass here and there, no fence of roses, no flower beds, not a single swing, no big rockers with comfortable cushions, just small plastic chairs. Had the house not been painted these many years?

On the far side of the fence where my mother grew her luscious strawberries and green asparagus, a corn field was now creeping past her garden to the lawn area.

I decided that I did not care to go inside. As we drove away, I looked back through my disappointment and despair. The old slate roof had been replaced. My beloved old home had a tin roof!

Was this really the same house where this little Country Girl grew up before she became a Southern Lady?

Part Three

*Life With a Passport –
International Traveler*

*Carolyne, the international traveler,
in Marrakech, Morocco.*

Trips of a Lifetime

A FTER Terry's father died, I said to her, "I've always wanted to travel abroad. It's a good time. Let's go."

She said, "I really don't want to go, but if you want me to go with you, I will." And so we went to Europe.

Terry had more fun than anyone else on the tour! On the way home, she asked, "Where are we going next year?"

We started traveling before I retired and continued traveling long after I retired. We toured Africa, Asia, South America, Australia, New Zealand, Eastern Europe, Western Europe; and cruised to the magical islands of the South Pacific, the Mediterranean, and the Caribbean.

Oh, I almost forgot, we traveled within our own country too. We visited so many memorable places, I can't recall them all. Fortunately, Terry has a photo album from each trip and has labeled every single picture she took. We have taken more than 35 trips, most of which have been international, including three trips around the world. Each one was the trip of a lifetime! This Southern Lady had become an International Traveler.

But, there are still more trips to take, and I still have more tales to tell...

Chapter 9
Trips to Europe

Exciting Expectations

ANTICIPATION of traveling to foreign places is almost as exciting as being there. I enjoy waking up in a strange room with its different types of furnishings: old-timey mattresses, sometimes hard lumpy ones; light fluffy pillows, and small hard ones. You can tell which part of the world you're in by the bed coverings that are in keeping with the decor of the area. Some are embroidered, some are eiderdown, some are lacy, some are tailored, and some look like tapestries. The bathrooms are even stranger. You need to be a genius to operate the shower.

I enjoy the strange breakfasts, very different from our Southern coffee and toast, or bacon, eggs, and grits. Most of the time, breakfast consisted of muesli, hard rolls, cheeses, and jam. In European countries, you have to add a half a cup of milk to drink their strong coffee.

I enjoy touring the cathedrals, basilicas, museums, and other points of interest in the cities. But even more, I enjoy the majestic scenery, the countryside, the charming villages, the native people—their customs, their dress, and their food. I enjoy arriving in a new place about twilight for an illumination tour, then picking out the places to visit the next day. I enjoy anticipating strange, exotic things.

Will tomorrow be even more exciting than my anticipation?

Oh, Henri

We were fortunate to have Henri with his 30 years of experience as our tour host on our first big trip. He was born in Poland, lived in England, and spoke seven languages fluently. This was one of those eight country tours. We were in France, the seventh country. It was one of the special nights with dinner at the Eiffel Tower. My small evening bag held very little. I hid my purse and locked my money and passport in the suitcase for safekeeping.

Our early departure for London the next morning required, "Bags out at 6:00 A.M." At the airport, our bags, unseen by us, passed customs as a group. As we stood in line for customs—*I remembered…*! I could just see my daughter, the group, and Henri in London, leaving me behind in Paris, with no money and no passport. We had constantly been reminded that the first commandment of tourism is to keep your passport with you at all times. With fear and trembling, I called, "Oh, Henri! My passport is in my suitcase."

To my surprise, Henri calmly said, "Carolyne, come with me." After a lengthy conversation between French officials and the tour host, I was allowed to leave France without a passport.

After we landed in London, the peace I had recently acquired had departed. How could I enter England without a passport? I frantically called, "Oh, Henri!"

Henri, in his usual manner, repeated, "Carolyne, come with me." I don't know what went on with the English people and him, but I was allowed into their country without a passport.

I couldn't erase from my mind that in a few days we would be leaving for home. Would they let me leave England as my passport did not show that I had ever entered it?

About that time, I saw the group baggage on a large cart and there was mine on the very bottom. Somehow, I found the courage to once again call, "Oh, Henri!" The baggage was unloaded and my suitcase pulled. I quickly unlocked it and retrieved my money and the passport. My daughter disowned me saying that she had never seen me before.

Back to the customs area Henri and I went to get the passport stamped. Now, I was legally in England. When my suitcase was pulled, I noticed that my brand-new bag was badly damaged. I didn't have the heart to tell the tour host, but Victoria, a tour mate, had also seen the damaged baggage and it was she who said, "Oh, Henri!"

The baggage had been reloaded with my bag on the bottom as before. Again, the 44 bags were unloaded. My bag, the porter, Henri, and I started the long trip to the damaged baggage claim department. The line was long. Henri left the porter and me with instructions as to where we were to meet the group. The bag was examined, I was asked for my ticket and passport, was handed forms to be mailed back, and was then dismissed.

When we returned, all 44 tour mates confronted me, "Show us the passport before you get on the bus."

Then, *I remembered...*! "Oh, Henri! The people in the claim department didn't return the passport to me." My feet and I were ready to cry.

Once more, the familiar voice simply said, "Carolyne, come with me."

Back down the corridor we went, around and about the detours because of the remodeling going on at Heathrow. It seemed like miles. But, even as we approached, the people in the claim department grinned and handed me the passport. As I boarded the tour bus, the applauding began.

After a full day of sightseeing, we arrived at the hotel about five o'clock. We were to go to dinner and the theater. I knew that the host would be happy to get rid of me, but as we waited for the room key, he approached my daughter and me saying one more time, "Carolyne and Terry, come with me and have a drink. You're such nice people."

The day I received a check from the airline, enough to pay in full for a brand-new bag, I wished that the tour host had been nearby. I would have called, "Oh, Henri!"

The Jewelry Shop

At an appointment with my podiatrist, I asked, "Can you do anything to help me because I have a trip to Europe planned and want to be able to walk in spite of an infected ingrown toenail?"

He asked me what countries I would visit and when I told him Italy was one of them, he asked which cities in Italy. When I mentioned Florence, he said, "I have a very good friend, Vincent, who owns a jewelry shop there. You must see his beautiful gold jewelry. He has the *finest* in all of Florence. And when you go, be sure and tell him my mother and I send our best regards and we're looking forward to a visit from them in the near future. Now, let me tell you where he's located," he said, pulling out his prescription pad.

He began to write and I began to worry because there was a room full of people waiting to see this doctor. Not only did he give me a shot to help my infected toe, but he also gave me directions to his friend's jewelry shop from various sites within Florence. I think it took three or four sheets from his prescription pad before he was through giving me directions.

When we arrived in Florence, the tour bus made a stop for anyone who wanted to go shopping. I looked at my directions and looked across the way. There was the Ponte Vecchio, the bridge where Vincent's shop was located. I told my tour mates that this shop had been recommended to me as having the *finest* gold in all of Florence, and invited the group to come with me. Away we went.

We walked for blocks passing intriguing shops and museums along the way. Finally, we arrived and found ourselves shaking hands with Vincent himself. I gave him the message from my podiatrist. He was so pleased. Eager to help us, he began to show us rings, bracelets, pendants, necklaces, earrings, and watches. We liked his jewelry, and decided it truly might have been the *finest* in all of Florence. But, the price of the jewelry might have been the *finest* in all of Florence too. After all our anticipation, excitement, lengthy directions, long walk, bypassing of other stores, and personal introduction, Terry and I were about to leave the jewelry shop empty-handed.

"What would you like to buy?" Vincent asked.

"I just want some black leather gloves," Terry answered.

Vincent said he had a friend who owned a leather store down the street and around the block and insisted on going with us to show us exactly where it was. We bade Vincent farewell with our *finest* Southern smiles.

Terry did not leave the leather shop empty-handed.

Our Dark Predicament

One day, on our first trip to Europe, we rode nine hours through spectacular scenery and arrived at a quaint hotel in Austria. That night, we attended a very entertaining folkloric dinner show. Even though it was after midnight when we returned to our room, Terry still had to shampoo and dry her long, black hair.

Forgetting that bathrooms in most European hotels were on a different electrical system from ours, she plugged in her hair dryer. Poof! The fuse had blown. Wartime blackout shades were still used over the windows, so we were in total darkness.

Feeling her way to the phone, Terry tried to dial the hotel operator. A sleepy voice of another hotel guest answered. After telling him of our dark predicament, she asked him to dial reception and have the hotel send help to our room. The guest gave a puzzling reply, "I can't, because I sleep in the nude," and hung up.

I crept to the door, opened it, and from the dim light of the hall, was able to find a robe. I remembered that one of our fellow travelers, Joyce, was staying across the hall from us. I knocked on her door and she readily agreed to get us some help. Then, she came to join us in our dark room.

A few minutes later, a strange character from the hotel arrived. His hair stuck out about six inches from all around his head. His long beard, bushy eyebrows, and other facial hair almost completely covered his face. We had to peer closely to find his eyes. However, the rescuer with his large flashlight was quite welcome. We did not speak his language, nor did he speak ours. He quickly assessed the situation and let us know by sign language that he would be right back. When he left, we fondly nicknamed him "Wooley Booger."

In just a few minutes, he returned with a new fuse and we had electricity. About that time, we had another visitor, his female assistant, with the same coiffure as our "Wooley Booger." She brought us an adapter so that the darkness would not occur again.

This strange gathering turned into a hilarious party. With gestures, sign language, and giggles, we all had quite a conversation. Even though it was after 2:00 A.M., our visitors seemed reluctant to leave. Terry did not have to use the hair dryer; her hair had dried on its own.

We never found out what sleeping in the nude had to do with dialing a telephone.

Enchanting Switzerland

After a typical Swiss breakfast of muesli, strong coffee that I had to fill with lots of hot milk, cheeses, breads, and jams, we left a delightful Swiss chalet high in the Alps. We journeyed through the majestic mountains, each view more exciting and beautiful than the one before. Even on this May morning, the snow was still measured in feet, not inches. After a leisurely drive through the constant grandeur and charming villages, we arrived at the foot of Mount Pilatus.

We left our Mercedes tour bus and driver and apprehensively climbed into a cable car to go to the top of the mountain. We could see the spring flowers, even the romantic edelweiss, in the meadows of the slopes below, and hear the tinkling cowbells as the shepherds moved their herds.

What a breathtaking view from the top! We felt like we were on top of the world. Never had a light lunch tasted so good: hot cocoa and hot, hot soup. The descent down the mountain was less scary, not so steep, with even more spectacular scenery. Then, we boarded a boat across the lake to Lucerne.

Our bus and driver awaited us for a tour of the city and shopping. Some of the group had joined this trip for the privilege of shopping at the many-storied Bucherer, with its expensive Swiss watches and other treasures at "so-called" discount prices. We enjoyed looking at the treasures, but waited to make our personal purchases elsewhere.

We visited the famous Lion Monument, and across the way was the shop that we had been awaiting. Their specialty was music boxes, the loveliest I had ever seen—some with intricate carvings, with graceful moving figures, with lilting tunes, with melodic tones—all sounding much like an orchestra. We bought these for family and special friends. It was at this shop that we purchased dozens of small souvenir cowbells for those who had requested we bring them something back.

The sun had begun to set as the bus delivered us to a

charming, renovated Swiss hotel, just in time to dress for dinner. To go to our restaurant for the night, we walked across Lucerne's famous, long, wood-covered bridge. The inside contained paintings on the wood from many artists. We were saddened when later we learned the bridge had burned. It was rebuilt, but could never recapture the original art.

Leaving the bridge, we were ready for the long-anticipated Swiss fondue dinner. Truly, it was worth waiting for. The folkloric show was most entertaining, with the yodeling, dancing, and strange musical instruments. The show ended with a musical salute to many different countries and states. It made us a little homesick when we heard "Georgia on My Mind."

But my mind was still on quaint villages, edelweiss, tinkling cowbells, and the majestic grandeur of the Swiss Alps!

The Lost Day

I was having my hair done early in the morning of the same day I was to leave on an overseas flight with Terry to begin a Mediterranean cruise. I told Alva, my hairdresser, "Yesterday, the strangest thing happened. The airport shuttle went to Terry's home and then came to my home to take us to the airport. We both told the driver that he had arrived on the wrong day and asked him to return today at eleven o'clock."

As I continued to talk about my travel plans, the lady in the next chair said, "Excuse me, I'm a travel agent. Would you mind my looking at your travel documents?" I handed them to her. In just a few seconds, she said, "Your plane left for Barcelona *yesterday!*"

I said, "Alva, please quickly hand me your phone!" I dialed Terry's number and told her that our plane had left the day before.

Terry replied, "I'll call."

I drove home as quickly as I could and called Terry again. Our travel agent had recommended that we go to the airport.

We had only a few minutes before the shuttle would pick us up. The cruise had already begun, we had missed our flight, our tickets were invalid, and we had no other plane reservations.

As soon as we arrived at the airport, Terry asked to speak to an airline manager while I waited with our baggage. The airline manager arranged for us to be on a flight leaving immediately. We flew to the airport nearest the city where our ship would be docked for the second day of the cruise.

The scenery on the hour drive from the airport to the cruise ship was astonishingly beautiful with the ocean, the beaches, and the French Riviera. We held our breath as the taxi sped around one hairpin curve after another! The driver meant for us to meet our ship before it sailed, and we did! Yes, we missed the boat, but only for the first day of the cruise.

We have *never, ever* missed the boat again!

Chapter 10
Trips to Asia

Surprise! Surprise!

WE were to take a cruise that departed from Dubai, where our travel package included two nights at a hotel. I thought it would be a simple lodge in the desert. *Surprise! Surprise!* We were taken to a magnificent five-star hotel.

As soon as we arrived, Terry headed for the restroom in the hotel lobby. The door had a painting of a long robe on it. As soon as she entered, an Arabic man entered as well. Insulted, she turned to face him. He was wildly gesturing and making motions she didn't understand. *Surprise! Surprise!* She was in the men's restroom. The only difference between the men's and women's restrooms was the color of the long robe painted on the door.

Next, we were taken to our room. *Surprise! Surprise!* We had a large bedroom with a television, a living room with an even larger television, and a kitchen also equipped with a television. They forgot to put a television in the bathroom.

We decided to see what was on each floor of the hotel. I remember the second floor. *Surprise! Surprise!* I thought I was in

Japan. There was a pagoda, many bonsai trees, and a stream of water flowing around jagged rocks with a charming bridge over it.

When we reached the top floor of the hotel, a man was standing at the door of a large room. When he saw us, he greeted us, "Come on in, come on in." He invited us to join the many people already comfortably seated, each smoking from a water pipe. The air had a sweet aroma. *Surprise! Surprise!* We were being invited to smoke what I thought was opium. Politely declining the invitation, we scurried to the elevator!

The next morning, we visited the shopping area beneath the hotel. *Surprise! Surprise!* It was a block-long shopping mall.

All too soon, we had to join our group to tour the city. *Surprise! Surprise!* The Arabs were very interested in education at all levels. We saw numerous academic buildings and a university with a beautiful campus.

On our return to the hotel, Terry said there was something she needed to do. She returned shortly with a huge smile. The hotel had given her a refill for their complimentary jar of fresh dates that she had long since devoured.

Somehow, I was *not surprised!*

The Trishaw Ride

We were so excited! We were in Singapore, known at the time as the cleanest city in the world. We would get to go to the famous Raffles Hotel, where the Singapore Sling originated. The first place on our tour was the botanical gardens, so tranquil and beautiful. Next, our tour included a trishaw ride. Now, I thought the trishaw would be a slow, easy ride through parks and gardens. Had I been fooled!

I climbed in the trishaw and before I could even get both my feet in, away we went—around the corners, in and out of traffic, dodging cars down the middle of busy streets. Horns beeped at my reckless driver, but he pretended not to hear them. He pedaled so fast, I couldn't see if the city was clean or not. I thought the trishaw was going to turn over. I didn't have a seat belt, but I sure did need one. I was scared to death! I wish I had walked!

When we all arrived at our destination, Terry said, "Mom, wasn't that fun?" She took one look at my face. She didn't need to hear me answer.

The First Time I Saw China

Shortly after the bamboo curtain was opened, our tour group of 44 people from all over the USA had the opportunity to board a local Chinese train in Kowloon to go into the New Territories. Our seats on this very ancient, slow-moving train were scattered among the locals. The well-worn, tattered, musty-smelling seats faced each other.

Not long after Terry and I took two seats facing forward, our local seatmates arrived. A hundred-year-old woman and her eighty-year-old son were returning home for the first time in some years. They were carrying all of their earthly possessions, which consisted of a pole with a large bundle on each end. The man was a little taller and a little leaner than most of the men of his culture. They both had on pajama-like outfits, worn by most of the peasants. Their piercing, small, slanting eyes didn't keep us from saying hello with a broad smile, which was acknowledged by a slight nod.

The ancient train groaned and chugged and finally began to creep along. But our adventure had already begun! We could tell from the woman's stooped shoulders, and the many, many lines on her face and neck, the kind of life she had endured. She began to fumble inside her top. I thought perhaps a strap had broken. Then, a look of relief appeared on her wrinkled, aged face. She had found the string for which she was searching.

Inch by inch, the string came into view. Then, a lump appeared. We were fascinated! The lump turned out to be a small bag. Opening the bag, she took out a vial. It was quite a feat for those gnarled fingers to get it uncorked. When she did, it was so potent, we could hardly breathe. We decided it must be for insect bites as she treated much of her anatomy. Finally, we were able to get the cantankerous train window open and welcomed the fresh air.

Scarcely had we settled back, when we heard a vendor coming. For the first time, Coca-Cola had come to China. Even though they spoke no English, our friends knew what it was and were about to have their first taste. They also knew it took money.

Again, the fumbling began for a different string. Those crippled fingers found it and slowly, slowly, out came another bag containing Chinese money. If Coca-Cola could have captured their expressions, they would have paid a tidy sum. The Chinese loved Coca-Cola!

The conductor came by and insisted that the aisles be kept clear. The Chinese man's menacing eyes seemed to spit fire as did his loud Chinese words as he defended his right to keep his possessions in his sight.

Never had we come face to face with such picturesque characters. I pointed to the camera protruding from my daughter's bag. She shook her head no. She was so wise.

Our tour friends, seeming to have business with us, just *had* to come by. When one venturesome gentleman's flash went off, the Chinese man knocked the camera from his hand while shouting strange Chinese words.

By now, the mother had problems again. Yes, the same procedure began—the string and the little bag. Inside was some sort of powdery substance. She doctored some more of her anatomy with it.

A look at the watch told us our interesting four-hour trip was nearing its destination. It had only seemed like minutes.

But not before the fourth string began to appear with its little bag. This time it contained some sort of edible seeds, which they shared and seemed to enjoy.

We bade our Chinese friends farewell. As we looked at some of the other local people departing, we were thankful for our colorful couple, instead of the one with the two live chickens and a small pig!

Buddha

How beautiful, how strange, how unusual, and how unique is the Orient—the topiary gardens, the pagodas, and the many Buddhas! I 'specially remember the Golden Buddha; it was the first one that we saw in one of the temples. I didn't realize that these statues were so large, but not too large for me to see signs saying "Contributions." So, I opened my purse and looked in my travel billfold—yes, I had quite a number of Oriental coins. I took them out and giving half to my daughter said, "Terry, we want Buddha to smile on us, so here's some coins for you to give to him."

As we went through the different Oriental countries, we saw many different Buddhas: the reclining Buddha, the sitting Buddha, the life-size Buddha, the largest Buddha, and lots of other Buddhas, always with the same sign. Each time, we went through the same procedure, with my giving Terry half of my coins to contribute to ensure Buddha would smile on us.

When we visited our last temple and I made my final contribution, I happened to see Terry putting the coins I had just given her into her pocket. I looked at her questioningly and asked, "Have you been pocketing the coins I've been giving you for Buddha all along?"

"Well, I need them more than Buddha does," she admitted.

As we left the temple, I noticed Buddha was no longer smiling!

Poverty and Riches

"Unless you can give to every one of the millions of beggars on the streets," our tour host warned us, "it's better to give to an organization that helps them help themselves." With these introductory words, our journey into India began.

Nowhere had we seen so much begging. Toddlers no more than two years old, people with one arm or leg, the elderly, and the hungry sleeping on the streets, all came to us with extended open hands. Yes, there were beggars and poverty, but there were also riches and beauty.

Very early in the morning, we were taken in a boat to observe the sunrise bathing rituals of the people gathered along the widespread steps descending into the Ganges River. The people bathed themselves as they greeted the rising sun. Following their custom, our guide floated a flower wreath in the river as a spiritual offering.

Later in the day, along the same edge of the Ganges, we watched funeral pyres being built for the cremation of the dead. The cremations were attended by family, friends, and passersby. Afterwards, the ashes were scattered in the Ganges, the same river where we had observed people bathing themselves earlier.

In Bombay (now Mumbai), we observed a different ritual for the dead belonging to a certain religious sect. At sunrise, the dead were placed on top of buildings with a flat top. The family and friends, dressed in their black funeral garb, waited below. The vultures would be circling above. By sunset, there would be no trace of the remains, not even the bones. This same sect did not believe in stepping on an ant. They wore a mask over their lower face to prevent harming even a gnat that might accidentally fly in their mouth.

So much of the lives of these people were lived outside their small one-room huts. From the rivers came almost all of the water for cooking, eating, drinking, cleaning, and washing clothes. Much to our surmise, the same rivers were used for bathing, brushing teeth, bathroom necessities, and other personal requirements.

Cows had the right of way on city streets as well as on country roads. Monkeys ran rampant. We could not put anything down, particularly food, because the monkeys would grab it and were gone before we could turn around. They also had the run of the temples.

I didn't dare take my eyes away from the windows of our tour bus. In a small village, I almost missed seeing a group of men from a sect marching down the street without even a fig leaf.

The women wore a sari even when they worked in the rice paddies. We were amazed how well the women were able to wrap one piece of material so that it always remained in place. The red dot that some wore on their foreheads, their nose rings, and their dangling earrings added to their intriguing appearance.

Before we reached any village, we could tell we were approaching one by the aroma. The spices that had been used so fluently in our food could be smelled at all hours from the outdoor cooking.

A walk through the spice gardens was most interesting. We saw big trees whose bark was dried and ground into an herb. All of us bought saffron because it was so inexpensive.

Off the southern coast of India, we visited the beautiful island country of Sri Lanka, where in Kandy, we saw a mile-long line waiting to see Buddha's tooth. On other parts of the island, we saw elephants pick up huge logs and carry them like a transport truck. From our tour bus, we watched the natives get in the rivers with these elephants to wash them with soap and brushes. The elephants, standing still, seemed to enjoy their baths.

To the east of India, we visited the mysterious country of

Nepal. In Kathmandu, we were told about the Living Princess. To be considered as the Living Princess, a young prepubescent girl can have no blemishes or marks anywhere on her body. She must spend the night alone and show no fear. When chosen, she leaves her family to live in a special dwelling with servants. We wanted to see her. After a lengthy wait outside her living quarters, she finally appeared at an upper window in full makeup. She flicked her long, dark hair in front of her shoulder, a gesture making her appear much more worldly than her young years. When any Living Princess reaches puberty, she returns to her previous status in life without servants. What an adjustment each one has to make!

I didn't see any white tigers, but I do remember the strange temples, the fragrant aromas, the ride on an elephant to see Amber Fort, the house in which Gandhi lived, the visit to the Taj Mahal, the air flight to see Mount Everest, the English tea plantations, and the beautiful sunsets of Sri Lanka.

These beguiling countries beckon me to return!

Making the Headlines

We had toured New Delhi, Jaipur, Agra, Sri Lanka, and Nepal, and were ready to tour the northern part of India, Srinagar. The hotel in Srinagar was quite different from a typical hotel. It was a houseboat on a lake with a houseboy, a sitting room, a dining room, and bedrooms, each with a small, pot-bellied stove. What a wonderful change from the heat to look out and see snow-covered mountains.

Our houseboy brought us meals from an off-site kitchen. He served them in the dining room on linen with china and crystal. Almost all the food, as was the custom in Srinagar, included so much curry that we tried to scrape it off.

After dinner, unexpected visitors arrived—vendors in boats bringing their wares to sell. We greeted them in the sitting room. Each had a different specialty you could buy: cashmere, spices, handmade carvings, crafts, hand-dyed silk, and woolen carpets. First, was the lady with hand embroidery. She passed her wares to each of us, hoping we would buy something. Then, the next visitor arrived, this time with jewelry. Last was our favorite, Cheap John. He brought a little of everything.

The evening became quieter when Cheap John left and we all retired. The houseboy had turned down the beds. We were asked who wanted the houseboy to keep the fire burning in their potbellied stove during the night. I didn't need any additional heat, but Terry, who was cold-natured, had already raised her hand. Several hours later, I heard a noise—it was the houseboy stoking the stove. I was sweating!

The next day, while sightseeing, our tour guide explained that during cold weather in Srinagar, the children wore a cape-like coat and carried pots of charcoal underneath them to keep warm. They never seemed to burn themselves. I just had to see one for myself. Children seemed to congregate in large groups, but I finally saw one little girl by herself. Understanding my request, she lifted her coat to show me her pot. In gratitude, I gave her a pen and some chewing gum. Suddenly, I was surrounded by throngs of children who seemed to come out of nowhere begging, "Chew gum! Chew gum! Chew gum!" Without enough gum for all of them, I had to flee from the circle that had besieged me. I was glad to return to the refuge of our tour bus.

All too soon, we were waving goodbye to our houseboy and were on our way to the airport to fly to New Delhi and then home. We boarded our plane and were scarcely off the runway when I looked out the window and noticed the propeller wasn't turning. We felt as if we were sitting in vibrator chairs. The snow-covered mountains seemed closer and closer. Why didn't the pilot turn away from the mountains? Why didn't we hear an announcement? We didn't know what was happening, but we knew it was serious.

Our tour host must have also sensed something was wrong. Sitting in front of us, he turned around and too calmly asked if we'd like a slice of his orange. Just as calmly, we shook our heads no.

"Terry, they'll never find our bones in these mountains of snow," I said.

"But Mom, we took out travel insurance. Diane will be rich!" Terry replied, referring to her sister.

About that time, we could feel the plane turning and descending. It returned to the airport. We landed in the middle of the runway and following instructions, we calmly evacuated the plane. Back to the houseboat we went to spend the night in Srinagar, still uninformed.

The next day, on another plane, we flew to New Delhi. When we landed, the first thing we did was find a newspaper. The newspaper stated that on an airline flight leaving Srinagar, 140 passengers panicked when one of the engines failed.

Panicked??? None of us even knew what had happened until we read about ourselves in the newspaper!

Chapter 11
Trips to Africa

The Tented Camp

Part of the planned itinerary of our safari in Africa was to spend one night in a tented camp surrounded by a strong wire fence. We had our own four-sided tent with twin cots. The back side of the tent had a large zipper. When we unzipped it, we could step through the zipper to access our own bathroom and shower area. This area consisted of three walls of cement blocks the same height as the tent, and was open to nature at the top.

The entire tour met at the lodge for the safari and for dinner before we retired to our respective tents. Outside the wire fence, we could hear lions roaring, hyenas laughing, and other animal sounds so close we thought they were about to enter our tent.

Terry unzipped the back of the tent and I heard her yell, "Mom, there is an insect 15 inches long over the toilet paper. What do I do?"

"Come on," I said, "I'll go with you." I followed Terry through the unzipped opening to the cement block stall. Then,

I panicked, screaming, "There's a bird flying in here!"

Terry pointed her flashlight and came eye to eye with the 15-inch-long insect and shrieked. She was terrified of insects and I was even more terrified of birds. We almost knocked each other down trying to get back into the tent. The zippered opening wasn't large enough for both of us at the same time.

We decided to sleep in our clothes. We heard scratching outside the tent. Just as I got to sleep, Terry woke me up, saying, "Something is scratching on my cot."

We looked at the mattress, on top of the mattress, underneath the mattress, took off the sheets, shook out the sheets, and remade the bedding. Then I asked, "Can I go back to sleep now?"

Hardly had I gotten to sleep again when Terry wailed, "There's still something scratching on my cot!" She was frantically examining her clothing to make sure no insects were on her. By now, sleep was hopeless for me.

It was a *lo-n-g* night. We heard scratching, roaring, and animal sounds until dawn. The loudest of all were the hyenas. We just knew they were laughing at us!

The Masai Offer

"Hurry and take your pictures," our tour guide told us when we visited a kraal of Masai in Africa. This kraal was a village of Masai people and their animals within a fence-like enclosure. The main food of the Masai was a mixture of milk and blood from their cows. Thank goodness these Masai were no longer one of the dangerous tribes!

Terry began snapping candid photos of the children, the elderly, the long multicolored beads they wore, and the bright cloth coverings many wore over their shoulders. While I watched the youngsters playing with the small animals, I couldn't help but notice a group of men surrounding a wise-looking older man who appeared to be the head of the tribe.

He held a long, wooden stick with a large, rounded knob at the top. Masai kept their sticks with them at all times. They used them for walking as well as a club to protect themselves from wild animals.

The head of the tribe began to eye my walking cane. I showed him that by pressing a button, like magic, it collapsed into a compact size. Then, by pressing the button a second time, it became a walking cane again. He had a broad grin on his face. He liked it! Thrusting his wooden stick toward me, he pointed at my cane. He wanted to trade. I laughed, then he laughed.

As the tour bus was leaving the kraal, Terry, who had been taking pictures of the ongoings, said, "Mom, why didn't you trade? You could have had a great souvenir!"

Can't you just see a Masai tribal leader trying to kill a ferocious lion with a collapsible aluminum cane?

Treetops

After lunch one day on one of our trips to Africa, the tour host said, "We have a treat for you. A famous witch doctor is here. Who would like to give him a few coins to have him tell your fortune?"

I raised my hand, and then began searching for the coins.

The witch doctor had penetrating eyes, held a crooked stick, and wore a loincloth. Since he spoke Swahili, he used an interpreter. The witch doctor looked at me and began talking. The interpreter told me that he had said I would return to Africa seven times.

I said, "Oh no, this is our last trip. We've already been here three times."

Instead of telling me of the great riches I would have, the witch doctor said I would never have much money, but I would always have enough. When he finished telling my fortune, other tour mates were eager to have theirs told as well, including

Terry.

The next stop was Treetops, where we arrived about three o'clock in the afternoon and could see a strange dwelling built on wooden stilts high in the trees. We could see steps leading to it. At the bottom of the steps stood a man dressed in military attire with a submachine gun in his hands and bullets lining the sash across his chest. As we approached, he told us in a commanding voice, "You *will not* come out of the building or down the steps until you officially depart from Treetops. If you drop anything, you *will not* come outside to get it. You *will* have tea on the top deck at four o'clock. You *will* eat dinner at six o'clock. You *will* depart tomorrow morning at nine o'clock. Are there any questions?" There was nothing but silence.

We went to our sparse room made of rough, unfinished wood like the rest of our hotel in the trees. We had two small cots and a mirror over a basin. There was so little space, we had to put our overnight bags on our cots. We were not allowed to bring a suitcase. Showers and toilets for the floor were down the hall. We had been told to latch the wooden shutter across the window or the monkeys that ran wild would come inside and explore our belongings. We washed our hands and left for tea on the open-air deck. We *were* there by four o'clock!

We sat in the fresh air talking with friends and enjoying refreshments. I put down my scone to drink my tea. I sensed movement and at that moment, Terry gasped. I saw a monkey scurrying away with my scone in his hand. The monkey had pushed Terry aside to get to it.

Before long, it was time for dinner and we *were* there at six o'clock, as we had been commanded. Dinner was served on a long, narrow table. Food was placed in bowls on a narrow board in the middle of the table. Guests served themselves and then pushed the entire board to the next person. Unfortunately, we were seated at the end of the table and had to wait quite a while for the board to reach us. The wait was worthwhile as the food was surprisingly good!

We then returned to the upper deck to view the animals. We looked out over a huge well-lighted pond and salt lick. Soon, elephants began to appear with several baby elephants among the herd. When wildebeests, zebras, or rhinoceros came too close, the adult elephants formed a circle facing outward with the baby elephants on the inside. The elephants didn't charge, but stayed in their formation protecting their young until the other animals moved farther away. I couldn't tear myself away from watching this fascinating sight beneath me.

When we went to our room, I immediately went to sleep. But, Terry stayed awake for hours watching the animals from our open window, hoping that a monkey would not climb through it and jump on her.

The next morning, there were no outside lights, no elephants, no animals of any kind. After breakfast, we made sure we *were* on time for the nine o'clock departure. I predicted the rest of the trip would be just as adventurous as Treetops.

I was right! And so was the witch doctor. I *did* return to Africa many times!

Chapter 12
Trip Memories

Because of Waiting

MANY times during our travels, when walking became too strenuous for me, I rested and waited while Terry and the tour group would sightsee or shop. My resting places included sitting on a wall, sitting in a restaurant, and sitting in a tour bus. Almost without fail, I had far more interesting and unusual experiences than they did.

While Terry shopped at the Plaka in Athens, Greece, I sat on a wall that surrounded a Greek Orthodox Church. Many well-dressed people began entering the Church. The women wore black high heels, black hose, and black gloves. The men had long black beards and wore black top hats. I tried to find out what was happening from the people around me, but they didn't speak English. Finally, an English-speaking lady explained that a funeral was being held for one of the highest priests of the Greek Orthodox Church.

After the funeral, his body was to be taken by boat for burial on an island off the coast of Greece. It wasn't very long before the funeral procession began. At least a dozen of the long-bearded men with top hats came out of the church, followed by an open casket. The casket was very narrow and shallow and shaped like a canoe. The priest in it wore many chains of gold as well as a gold cross around his neck. His headdress was bedecked with many jewels.

Because of waiting, I had just had my first opportunity to see a funeral procession for a high priest of the Greek Orthodox Church.

While Terry climbed the Great Wall of China, I waited for her and the rest of the tour group at a small restaurant. I sat at a table near a window where I could view the Great Wall. A waiter asked for my order and I told him I just wanted some hot tea. Before my cup was half empty, a second waiter approached and asked if I wanted anything else. After a few more sips of tea, a waitress approached me. She asked if I'd like a refill. After a second waitress came and left, I wondered why four different people had been so attentive to me over one cup of tea. Then a fifth person approached me. He chuckled and said, "Hello, I'm the manager. There will be no charge for your tea. You may not know it, but my staff has been practicing their English with you. Thank you for your politeness and kindness to them."

Being a Southerner, I simply smiled and said, "Y'all are so welcome." After the manager left, even more waiters and waitresses came to speak to me.

Because of waiting, I had just had my first opportunity to help these Chinese practice speaking English in *my Southern style*!

While Terry and the tour group were on a walking tour in Israel, I waited in the tour bus. The driver told me of a nearby shop that sold woodcarvings and other special souvenirs. Now, I love woodcarvings and told him I would like to go. With no crowds and no hurry, I shopped and I chose and I bought. After returning to the bus, the driver brought both of us a cup of tea. While I was shopping, a very generous offer of live camels was being made in exchange for Terry. I understood the offer was almost twice what was offered in exchange for a famous actress.

Because of waiting, I had just *missed* my first opportunity to exchange my daughter for live camels. But, I really didn't need any more camels; I had just finished buying some hand-carved ones!

Unforgettable People

We've met many unforgettable people in our travels…

— Roger, a New England college professor, who at the most famous, historic places, always asked where the shops were;
— Hans, the Swedish playboy, who made a living escorting ladies;
— Robert, who bemoaned the fact his beloved roommate, Mr. Smith, was unable to accompany him on the trip. Mr. Smith wrote us months later that Robert had died;
— Bob, who was looking for a seventh wife;
— John, who was held hostage in Beirut for over a year and used the paper and pen he was given to make himself a deck of cards to keep his sanity;
— a millionaire couple from California, who bought anything, everything, from anywhere, everywhere. They later flew in their own plane to visit us;
— Frank, a school principal, and Joyace, his wife, from Lake George, New York, who visited us five times;
— Wally and Sue, morticians from Spokane, who also have visited us;
— Dear Byron, a thirty-year-old retired attorney, with fiancées in five different cities, who visited us twice;

…along with many other memorable people.

The person who was most unforgettable was raised in Africa with a chimpanzee for a brother. Dr. Peacock was my seatmate on a return flight from Greece. He was an older man who had just married his surgical nurse. On this long trip, he told me about his childhood. As a lonely, only child, a young chimpanzee was adopted for him as a playmate. The chimp shared their home, ate with them, and slept in his other twin bed. Dr. Peacock's new wife was as interested in his story as was I.

We were interrupted by lunch, after which my interesting companion decided to take a nap. I could hardly wait for him to wake up. Perhaps my squirming helped rouse him. First, I wanted to know how the chimp ate. Could he use a spoon? No, I was told that he ate like most small children, with his fingers. He sat in an old high chair and wore a bib.

My intriguing companion seemed to be napping again, but my thoughts were of that family in Africa. I had learned his father was a doctor, his mother a teacher. As a boy, he was homeschooled and was sent to England for college and medical school, returning home to Africa for summer vacations. My seatmate and his wife now lived in Alabama and raised peacocks to match their name.

We had refueled in Newfoundland and were headed for home. Later, the captain announced we would land in Atlanta in less than an hour. My seatmate stirred. I just had to have one more question answered. How did they handle the chimp's bathroom activities? Why, of course, the chimp wore the African version of Pampers.

As we said goodbye at the airport, he handed me his card and invited me to visit them at Peacock Acres. I certainly would like to—I have many more questions that need answers!

Bizarre Cuisines

I enjoy tasting different foods in different countries. Perhaps the strangest food I ever tasted was monkey brains, served to me in Morocco. The looks alone were enough to make Terry turn her head in disgust. They looked exactly like a brain, lines and all, and tasted like nothing I've ever tasted before.

I have tried crocktail, a cocktail made from crocodile tail that looked and tasted a little like pork. I have also tasted conch in the Bahamas and blood sausage in Argentina. Though less adventurous, I enjoyed the cheese blintzes and borscht in Russia, the cheese fondue in Switzerland, the paella in Spain, moussaka in Greece, seafood in Chile, and high tea in England. The strangest breakfast I ate was in the Orient, vegetables and salad, which I normally eat for lunch.

But undoubtedly, the most unusual meal I've ever had was Peking duck. First, the waiter showed our table a brown, roasted duck on a platter. I expected to have a slice of duck brought to me; instead, the first course was the crisp, brown skin of the duck topped by a brown sauce and leeks, placed in a thin pancake, then rolled into a cylindrical shape. Next, we were served duck soup made from the bones of the duck. Then, we were served sliced duck with rice, salad, side dishes, and dessert. Each of the courses was served in an individual dish.

Now, this meal was served to a group of 12 people. By the end of the meal, we calculated that approximately 144 individual dishes would have to be washed in addition to our silverware and all the cooking pots. I'm glad I didn't have to wash dishes! There was plenty of hot green tea, but we couldn't seem to get bottled water, ice water, or even tap water.

Yes, I'm an adventurous eater, but I have to admit, even I wouldn't taste the worm sandwiches sold at the bullfights in Spain!

Unique Bathrooms

We have visited almost 100 countries throughout the world and many had different types of bathrooms.

The Orient had the most unique toilets of all. I thought the days of privies and using Sears Roebuck catalogs for toilet paper were long gone until I went to the Orient. Some of their toilets were just a hole in the floor with two boards on either side; others were just a hole in the floor. I had to bend, squat, balance, and aim to use them.

Then, there were the toilets in the European countries. I never knew how to flush them. Do I push, pull, or turn the knob, the chain, or the button? The search for toilet paper would begin. Whenever toilet paper was available, the texture ranged from a paper bag to sandpaper. I quickly learned to carry tissues with me at all times.

Next, came the bathing experiences. Which of the multiple controls do I use? How do I get hot water? Do I press the red switch, lift the blue handle, or turn the silver dial? Would the water come out of the hand-held sprayer, the shower nozzle, or the bath faucet? Inevitably, I would call my daughter, "Terry, I can't get the shower to come on!" It took both of us to figure out how to bathe.

Often, it was hard to tell which was the bath mat and which was the towel. But, I could tell in Scotland. They had oversized towels almost as big as blankets hanging on heated towel rods. Nothing felt so good on cold, damp days as those warmed towels.

Yes, many bathrooms throughout the world have been challenging, but fortunately only one experience was actually frightening: sharing a bathroom with our worst phobias, an erratic bird and a gigantic insect, in the tented camp in Africa!

The Maharani

After traveling through India and Nepal, I was getting ready for my first day of returning to work. I decided to make this day a memorable one. I put on a headdress, a red dot on my forehead, and a ring in my nose. A large shawl completed my outfit.

As I entered the building, my manager insisted he needed to talk with me in his office right away. He had changed a number of accounting procedures while I was gone and wanted to tell me about them. As we reviewed his changes, he began to laugh. "It's very difficult to talk with you with that ring in your nose," he said.

"I had planned to greet my coworkers first, then remove all traces of India before I met with you," I explained. He agreed to finish the talk later, so off I went to astonish my friends at work.

When I saw my first coworker, she insisted on leaving her office to watch the other coworkers' reactions. The next coworker did the same until an entire group was listening to me tell about my trip and drinking the tea I had brought them as a souvenir from India. After sharing a few tales, I removed my Indian garb and went to my office.

Carolyne, the maharani, had to return to her life as Carolyne, the corporate accountant!

Haggling

Many vendors in foreign countries raise the prices of their souvenirs expecting you to haggle. Tour mates and I have compared the price we have paid for the same souvenirs from the same vendors. They were astonished that I paid a much lower price than they did. Many have asked me how I haggle.

First, I always carry American dollars in small denominations for haggling. I usually take 100 one-dollar bills as well as some five-, ten-, and twenty-dollar bills with me on every trip. Most vendors want American dollars. Then, I decide how much I want to pay for a souvenir, but I offer a much lower price for it. When vendors don't lower their price, one technique I use is to hold up the cash in my hand for the exact amount I want to pay. After seeing the cash, the vendor often accepts my offer.

When vendors don't lower their prices to ones that are acceptable to me, I simply walk away. Sometimes, the vendor follows me. After I walked away from one street vendor who did not lower his price, he followed me several blocks to my tour bus. When I was seated on the bus and the bus slowly began to move, I pulled the amount of money I wanted to pay for the item out of my purse and showed it to the vendor from the bus window. With the bus still in motion, I lowered the window, the vendor handed me the object, grabbed the money, and quickly walked away.

I have some fascinating souvenirs: a thangka from Nepal; a six-foot-long scroll from China; a Koran holder; a wooden replica of St. Basil's Cathedral in Moscow; an antique cosmetic holder from Nepal; a beaded wedding necklace from Africa; a cartouche from Egypt; replicas of a terra cotta soldier and a horse from Xi'an in China; a Maltese Cross pendant from Malta; a glass replica of a mosque from Turkey; pictures from England; a hand-painted bowl from France; a leather purse from Morocco; kente cloth from Ghana; a wooden mask from Fiji; a cinnabar vase from China; a painted wooden Dala horse from Sweden; a replica of a wooden cart from Costa Rica; an embroidered tablecloth from Hong Kong; a straw basket from Ecuador; spices from the island of Grenada; worry beads and vases from Greece; an olive wood Bible from Jerusalem; a Majorca pearl pendant from Spain; a shrunken head from South America; and numerous figurines and carvings from Thailand, Africa, Spain, Greece, Colombia, Argentina, Denmark, and

Egypt.

I bought most of these through haggling!

My Collections

On our first trip to Europe, at St. Paul's Basilica in Rome, I saw the largest, most impressive candlestick I'd ever seen. It was about 15 feet high. While roaming their gift shop, I found a small replica of it. Exchanging my lira for this fascinating souvenir began what is now my collection of approximately 50 candlesticks.

The sizes and shapes of these candlesticks are varied. The hand-carved ones from Africa include a native profile and a lion with tiny teeth. I have an engraved pewter one from Morocco, a glazed ceramic one from Puerto Rico, a shell one from Tahiti, and colorful hand-painted ones from Mexico. I also like the colonial and Early American ones from New England. My candlestick collection sits on a hand-carved seventeenth-century buffet.

I also collect plates from countries I visit. Some are brass, metallic, pottery, sculpted, wooden, painted, or hand-carved. Others depict scenes from Corsica, Italy, Germany, Fiji, and Alaska. The ones from Romania, Turkey, and Morocco have designs all over them. I even have one with an Irish blessing on it. I display all of my plates on a wall.

I find myself looking for collectibles whenever I take trips. I must confess—one of the reasons I love to travel to new places is so that I can add to my collections.

The Greatest of These

I've seen many wonders of the world. I've...

— seen the Great Pyramids;

— cruised the Nile with its mysteries;

— observed the giant statues at Abu Simbel;
— visited the famous mud baths with their curative powers at the Dead Sea;
— stood at the Masada and marveled at the courage of the Jewish people during the battle which took place on that mountain;
— passed through the narrow opening into the valley at Petra, observing the families still living in its ancient caves;
— flown to see Mount Everest, the highest mountain in the world;
— been almost close enough to touch wild lions and elephants in Africa;
— set foot on the Great Wall of China;
— breathed the horrible dust to observe the hundreds of life-size terra cotta figures guarding the tomb of China's emperor;
— enjoyed the graceful beauty of Japan with its temples and pagodas;
— seen the many different Buddhas of the Orient;
— viewed the nearly mile-long line of people waiting to see the sacred tooth of Buddha in Sri Lanka;
— observed, from a point on the southern tip of South Africa, the different colors of the waters where the Indian Ocean meets the Atlantic Ocean;
— trod some of the paths of Jesus in Jerusalem, Nazareth, and Caesarea;
— crossed the Sea of Galilee to the Golan Heights with machine guns surrounding us;
— passed by the Church of Multiplication, where the feeding of the multitudes with the loaves and fishes occurred;
— been in the largest mosques, cathedrals, and basilicas in the world;
— seen the early diggings of the Incas in Machu Picchu;
— visited the spot where Stanley found Livingstone;

— viewed the mighty Victoria Falls;
— entered a kraal of the Masai, where milk and blood from their cattle are mixed for their primary food;
— watched the changing of the guard at Lenin's Tomb in Red Square in Moscow;
— been in many palaces and castles of kings and feudal lords of Europe and Asia;
— watched the old men of Greece finger their worry beads while I admired the whitewashed beaches of their islands;
— visited the ancient ruins of Athens, Rome, and Istanbul;
— seen the greatest of art in Paris, Rome, London, Florence, and Spain;
— seen the Taj Mahal at midnight;
— watched the sunrise rites of the Hindus on the Ganges;
— seen the cremations and scattering of ashes into the Ganges, and from the same river, watched the people dip into jugs what they believed to be holy water, carrying them on their heads and walking as far as 50 miles to their villages;
— seen my daughter kiss the Blarney Stone in Ireland;
— watched lace being made by hand in the ancient city of Brugge;
— observed the midnight sun in the northernmost part of Europe;
— seen many different brightly painted Hummel statues on the streets of Hamburg;
— toured Amsterdam from a boat winding through the many canals;
— explored the charming city of Honfleur, France, rightly named for its flowers;
— watched the native dancers in Tahiti;
— eaten pineapple out of the field on the Big Island of Hawaii;
— stood on the deck of a cruise ship at night watching a volcano spew out its flaming lava, as it flowed down the

mountain into the ocean, filling our lungs with its fumes;
— enjoyed watching the native people in Mexico and Central America creating their many Aztec crafts;
— liked the unusual coastal sights in Halifax, including the lighthouse used as a post office at Peggy's Cove;
— met in Goa the little girl from India that my daughter sponsored through ChildFund International;
— been invited to join in the smoking of what I thought was opium through the water pipes at a five-star hotel in Dubai;
— been pleased to see the modern university campus and academic buildings in the United Arab Emirates;
— been surprised to see the tallest building in the world at the time in Kuala Lumpur;
— observed the hurry-scurry of the South Korean citizens;
— held on for dear life in a trishaw in Singapore;
— eaten lunch like Hemmingway at the famous Raffles Hotel in Singapore;
— dined high above Paris at the Eiffel Tower;
— survived passing immigrations in England without a passport;
— ridden a camel and watched the mysterious veiled ladies in Morocco;
— enjoyed dipping into the famous fondue in Switzerland;
— viewed the breathtaking scenery and snowcapped Alps in Switzerland;
— been apprehensive as the Kenyan witch doctor, wearing only a loincloth, holding his crooked stick, speaking Swahili, told my fortune prior to going to the famous Treetops for the night;
— had a monkey push my daughter aside to steal my scone laying on a napkin beside me while on the observation deck of Treetops;
— been saddened by the extreme poverty of Benin, Togo, and Abidjan in Western Africa;

— worn a miner's hat going down and through the dim underground diamond mines in South Africa;

— seen the tented homes of the nomads, deep in the Sahara
Desert;

— thought that the tall, colossal dunes in the Namibian Desert were as alluring as those in the Sahara;

— landed at night in Hong Kong, with the light reflecting all
around the water, looking like a fairyland;

— been a passenger aboard a Boeing 737 airplane that lost
an engine taking off from the mountains of Srinagar and
wondered if we would lose our lives;

— read the following day's newspaper report that 140 "panic-
stricken" passengers and crew were safely evacuated from
a Boeing 737 airplane;

— glided in a gondola through the narrow canals of the romantic city of Venice, while being serenaded by our gon-
dolier;

— seen blue starfish and many other brightly colored fish
while snorkeling in the Great Barrier Reef off Australia's
shores;

— watched the Whirling Dervish, known as Sufi, make a rare
dancing appearance in Konya, Turkey;

— experienced the taste of monkey brains, conch, and crocktail;

— marveled at the size and brilliance of the crown jewels in
London;

— joked with the Beefeaters at the Tower of London;

— been awed with reverence by viewing the Pieta;

— applauded the festive parade of matadors and picadors at
the bullfight in Madrid, Spain, but cringed at the killing of
the bulls;

— walked through the dim, curving alleys of the mysterious
souks, with venders selling spices, leather, and handiwork
in Turkey and Morocco;

— ridden the Bullet Train in Japan and the luxurious Blue Train in South Africa;
— seen the young Living Princess in Kathmandu, chosen for her perfect body and bravery;
— glided in a boat through the dark Waitomo Caves of New Zealand, lit by thousands of glowworms clinging to the walls;
— observed the fairy penguins waddle from the sea to feed their young on shore in Australia;
— felt like a maharani, riding an elephant to see the Amber Fortress in Jaipur, India;
— watched the exotic burst of sunrises and the mellow glow of sunsets and their reflections in the ocean below, from a cruise ship in the middle of the South Pacific.

St. Paul concludes a well-known passage in the Bible, "…and the greatest of these is Love."

To return home to the USA with its freedoms, to family and friends, to the black dirt of South Carolina, to the red clay of Georgia, to Atlanta, and to my own great big comfortable bed—*this is the greatest of these*!

Part Four

Life Among Relatives –
Legacy of Memories

Carolyne and her siblings. From left to right –
Back row: Carolyne, Vernon, Helen.
Front row: Kent, Jimmy, Gray.

The Family

My Paternal Grandparents
Clara Pevey Taylor
William Henry Taylor

My Maternal Grandparents
Martha Hettie Spilliards Gray
William Frank Gray

Memorable Relatives
Lillie Gray Thomas
Thomas Lincoln Taylor
John Herbert Pettigrew

My Mother and My Father
Lula Annie Gray Taylor
Heyward Marable Taylor

My Sister and My Brothers and Me
(in order of birth)
Helen Marjorie Taylor
Vernon William Taylor
Carolyne Antoinette Taylor
Gray Heyward Taylor
James Franklin Taylor
Richard Kent Taylor

My Husband
Herbert Ray Wynne

My Children

(in order of birth)
Diane Wynne Norris
Steven Duane Wynne
Terry Lynne Wynne

My Grandchild

Heather Elizabeth Norris

My Great Grandchild

Rylan James Ricard

Chapter 13
My Grandparents

My Paternal Grandparents

MY paternal grandmother, Clara Pevey Taylor, was a schoolteacher. My paternal grandfather, William Henry Taylor, was a highly respected judge. They had eleven children including Thomas Lincoln Taylor, my favorite uncle.

In Ridgeland, South Carolina, my grandparents owned the Sycamore Hotel, a restaurant, and a general store, all facing the railroad depot. Sometimes, my mother worked in their general store, which sold everything from shoes to horse collars. After I was married but before I had children, I kept the hotel for my grandparents to go on vacation, which was usually twice a year.

The hotel was named after the huge sycamore tree shading the front porch. Across the street from the hotel was a park in which my grandparents built a gazebo and walking paths. This park was named Sycamore Park, after the hotel.

I especially remember my grandparents' bedroom in the hotel. There was no central heat, but a fireplace with grates to burn coal. It became a family sitting room in the winter as well as a sleeping room for them. It always smelled of "Twenty-three," a very pungent medication, good for what ails you.

I loved to eat in the restaurant with my grandparents. Instead of serving family style like most restaurants of the time, Hattie, the cook, served the food in individual dishes for each person. I can still smell the enticing aroma of the country steak and gravy.

Very often after supper, in back of the hotel, we children would play "tin can." Someone would hit a tin can and whoever was "it" would have to retrieve it while the other players ran and hid. We thought it was great fun.

In the summertime, all of us family and friends would sit on the hotel porch. Sometimes in the afternoon, when my aunts were visiting their parents, they would get lime sherbet and pour ginger ale over it. This was so refreshing!

When I was about eight, my Aunt Bea, my father's youngest sister who was postmistress, would pick me up at the hotel and take me with her to the post office less than two blocks away. She let me turn the handle of the machine that stamped the mail. That made me feel so important!

My grandparents were very kind to me. I remember them taking my cousin, Toxey, and me to Georgia—to Tybee to go swimming, and also to Quitman and Ludowici to meet my grandmother's relatives, the Peveys. When I was a small child, my grandmother even showed me how to iron her linen handkerchiefs. Many times, she gave me her best advice, "If you want anything bad enough, try hard enough, wait long enough, if it is right for you, you will achieve it."

My grandparents had many drummers (traveling salespeople) who stayed at the hotel several times a month as well as regular boarders. One of these boarders was a dancing teacher. She was very petite and not too young. Things did not go well with her and she had become several months behind in paying her bill.

When I was thirteen years old, to defray the dancing teacher's bill, my grandparents decided I should take tap dancing and ballroom dancing lessons. Two other teens and I would have to walk the two miles into town on an unpaved, dusty road to take the lessons. Arriving tired and sweaty, can't you see us trying to learn to ballroom dance? I don't think we can completely blame the teacher for us not becoming as adept and graceful as we should have. I was never able to take enough lessons for her to pay her bill, to my grandparents' chagrin.

Even though my grandparents had over twenty grandchildren, they always made me feel as if I was their favorite!

Grandmother Taylor, at the age of seventy-four, left us in the year of 1940.

Grandfather Taylor, at the age of seventy-eight, left us in the year of 1944.

My Maternal Grandparents

I never knew my grandfather, William Frank Gray. His first wife had died, so I never knew her either. They had one child known to us as Aunt Lillie.

After my grandfather's first wife died, he married my grandmother, Martha Hettie Spilliards, whom I did know. She was born in Bluffton, South Carolina, and was very young when they married. I remember the black velvet ribbon with the cameo she always wore around her neck. Her hair was never cut; she wore it in a bun on the nape of her neck. She made silk quilts for most all the girls and women in our family, including me. She taught me how to embroider and make French knots.

Grandfather Gray was a profitable farmer and owned much land as well as a cotton gin, a gristmill, a country store, a sawmill, a blacksmith shop, and a turpentine plant. People in his area who needed anything would say, "Let's go to Gray's." Today, in honor of my grandfather, a small town in the same location where he lived in lower South Carolina is named *Grays*.

My grandparents had two boys and four girls, including my mother, Lula Annie, and her sister, Clifton Carolyn, a pretty, tall, blue-eyed blonde for whom I was named. Their other girls were Pearl and Gladys, and the boys were Lewis and Ruth. Pearl worked for the Jacksonville Chamber of Commerce in Florida, and Gladys married the attorney who helped her get a divorce from her first husband. After Clifton Carolyn divorced the Englishman who kidnapped my brother, Gray, she later married the United States Junior Surgeon General.

My Grandfather Gray died of a heart attack, leaving my Grandmother Gray financially well off, but sadly, all was lost in the stock market crash of 1929.

Grandmother Gray, at the age of seventy-nine, left us in the year of 1947.

Grandfather Gray, at the age of fifty-three, left us in the year of 1907.

Chapter 14
Memorable Relatives

Aunt Lillie

I remember Lillie Gray Thomas, my Grandfather Gray's child from his first marriage. She was the best cook in the world. When she made toast, she even took time to spread the butter to the crust on both sides of the bread. After having poor sight for some years, Aunt Lillie lost all of her sight. She couldn't tell night from day.

One time, I visited Aunt Lillie at the Baptist Village in Waycross, Georgia. When she was told who I was, she arose gracefully from her chair and hugged me. Then, starting at the top of my head, she began to "see me." I realized as her fingers moved over my face, the cheekbones, the ears, the lips, down my arms, and around my waist, that she could tell many things: wrinkles, weight loss or gain. I think she could even determine the state of my health and whether I was happy or sad.

Her lunch was brought in and I marveled at her ability to tell how hot her coffee was, and where the meat as well as other food was on her plate. She explained that the same type of food was always put in the same place on the plate, like numbers on a clock dial. She didn't spill a single thing.

I noticed the family portraits and some other familiar things that I had seen over the years. She too must have been aware of them. I left with a good feeling. She escorted me to the door, not bumping into a single object. Now I understand how the blind can see!

Lillie Gray Thomas, at the age of ninety-four, left us in the year of 1977.

My Favorite Uncle

I remember Thomas Lincoln Taylor. Since both my mother and father were among the eldest of their respective families, I had some young, unmarried aunts and uncles. My very favorite uncle was Lincoln, who was quite handsome. He was a college professor who taught physics at The Citadel in Charleston, South Carolina, and later became a pilot. There weren't very many people interested in aviation in those days.

When visiting us, he would fly over our house and drop a note tied to a weight of some kind telling us when and where to pick him up when he landed. There was no airport in Ridgeland, so we would have to go to Savannah to meet him.

It wasn't very long after he became a pilot for Uncle Sam that he made the headlines on the front page of the newspapers: "South Carolina Native Flies Generalissimo Chiang Kai-shek and China's Gold." I don't remember from where to where; I was too young.

On his way home from China by ship, Lincoln met a young lady, Martha, from Oregon. She had been given a trip around the world by her parents as a college graduation present. She followed Lincoln to Ridgeland and in less than a year, they were married, the result of that shipboard romance. Even though they built a house next door to my family, they didn't live there long before moving to Baltimore for my uncle to return to his career in aviation. They took with them their new young son, Thomas Roland Taylor.

Uncle Lincoln, at the age of seventy-five, left us in the year of 1981.

Little Bert

I remember John Herbert Pettigrew, my nephew, the son of my husband's sister, Lillian. Weighing about five pounds at birth, this weak, premature baby boy was often sick. His frail body offered little resistance to colds, congestion, and pneumonia. He constantly struggled to live.

At that time, there was no central heat, just a potbellied stove to be stoked 24 hours a day. That particular winter was very bitter. Thinking it was the right thing to do, the baby was kept in a small, hot room, which was a hindrance to his breathing. He was held almost all of the time, not given a chance to even whimper, much less cry to develop his lungs. I remember old Dr. Ryan saying, "You're killing this baby with kindness."

This little, weak, spindly fellow developed into a normal, handsome, young boy with big brown eyes, golden curly hair, and a ready smile that charmed everyone with whom he came in contact. He was called Little Bert.

He decided big people weren't nearly as much fun as little people. He enjoyed his playmates and would give them his nice toys to take home for keeps. He became the whole community's little darling, loved by old and young alike, but truly worshiped by his mother and grandmother.

This little boy was interested in everything and everybody. It seemed that every minute had to be lived to the fullest; each sunbeam had to be captured. He even hated to stop to go to sleep, afraid that he might miss a new experience.

When he was almost four, Little Bert bumped his knee, which became infected and did not heal. After a long, painful stay in a children's hospital, he was diagnosed as having osteosarcoma, cancer of the bone. The doctor advised his parents to take him home, keep him comfortable with medication, and make him as happy as possible.

When he was five, he had two goals for his life. The first was to start school in September and be with other children all day. The second was to go camping in a tent with his playmates. A small tent was pitched on his grandparents' big screen porch, where Little Bert and his friends often went camping and had many adventures.

Little Bert put up a good fight, but the cancer wracked his body. This brave little fellow would ask for something to bite on so he would not cry out loud when the pain became severe.

He didn't get to enter the 1st grade. In September, before the first day of school, my nephew was laid to rest in a small South Carolina cemetery under a canopy lettered with his name on it. For many years, a canopy was kept over his grave. It gave the family much comfort to think of it as a tent for him to continue his camping. Each time the canopy was replaced, it was always lettered the same—Little Bert.

Little Bert, just 26 days before he was the age of six, left us in the year of 1939.

Chapter 15
My Mother and My Father

My Mother

I remember my mother, Lula Gray Taylor, one of six children. I wish I had been there to see my very prim, conservative, moral, virtuous mother after her marriage to my adventurous, happy-go-lucky, high school dropout, entrepreneurial father, leave for their honeymoon on a motorcycle with a sidecar. After my older sister was born, my mother, with the new baby in the sidecar of the motorcycle, went with my father to trade it in for their first car—a Model T Ford!

I've never heard of anyone who didn't like my mother. She was thoughtful, loving, unassuming, kind, and caring, though she didn't always show it through hugs and kisses. She was a no-frills person, always striving for harmony. She was the pillar of strength and stability of our family.

My mother taught me so much: crocheting, knitting, cleanliness, organization, the importance of good reading, and love of family. I would like to have the recipes she kept in her head, especially the ones for floating island, cracker and cheese casserole, and turkey dressing. There are so many questions I would like to ask her.

I remember the time when special overnight company was due any minute. One of my father's hounds used the guest bed for the bathroom. This was one of the few times I saw my mother cry.

My mother had a small vegetable garden beside the house. She grew carrots, tomatoes, lettuce, green and red bell peppers, strawberries, and even asparagus, which was quite hard to grow. She made her own fresh mayonnaise. For dessert, she made hand-churned strawberry-custard ice cream from her homegrown strawberries as only my mother could make it!

I remember how she liked fresh-cut flowers in the house. On the day she died, she had been outside early that morning cutting flowers and making arrangements inside. Then, she went back outside to trim around the trees in the places the lawn mower couldn't reach. It was there that a passerby saw her crumpled, lifeless body. With her passing, the weekly family gatherings for Sunday dinner ended and we never regained the family closeness again.

My mother, at the age of fifty-six, left us in the year of 1949.

My Father

I remember my father, Heyward Marable Taylor, the oldest of eleven children. It was not surprising to hear that he did not return to school after the 8th grade, but left home to be on his own. After working a short time on the railroad, nothing seemed too big for him. He was even a deputy sheriff.

I never saw my father hammer a nail, cut a piece of wood, or do any kind of physical labor. He made a living in road construction and built the basic foundation for more roads in South Carolina than anyone else at that time. He would go to Columbia, the state capital, and submit his bid on the particular roads in which he was interested. The lowest bidder would get the contract. How my father could tell what to bid puzzled me.

These new roads would go through the forests and hills and pastures and swamps. Dirt would have to be moved from the hills to the swamps, with ditches dug to drain the lowlands. When all was done, the roads had to be as smooth as a bed-sheet in preparation for paving.

For a time, one of his brothers, Lincoln, who had been a professor of physics at The Citadel in Charleston, worked with him. My father, a self-made man, could outfigure his learned brother. It was my father who made the monumental calculations enabling him to bid on these roads.

Aside from making a living in road construction, my father ran a large farm, raising cattle and hogs and the food for them. He could look at a field of corn and tell you how many bushels it would yield.

He was a wheeler-dealer, knowing how to take little things and make them into big ones. He could make money, but not save it. If it hadn't been for my mother, I don't know how things would have been.

My father certainly was a busy man with the road construction and the farm, but not too busy to read three newspapers each day. He knew more people than any other person I know. My mother never knew how many people she would be feeding at mealtime or whether she would be feeding a senator, a wealthy man, a fox hunting friend, or a derelict. It didn't matter to my father.

My father never lost his love for building roads, riding, hunting, fishing, or the farm. He loved that farm! After he quit doing these things, it seemed as if he lost his love of living.

My father, at the age of sixty-four, left us in the year of 1955.

Chapter 16
My Sister and My Brothers

Helen

Iremember my sister, Helen Marjorie Taylor Sullivan Ingram. My sister Helen, the oldest of the six of us, never liked me very much. But I didn't like her either—until she went to college. She was almost six years old when I was born and my brother Vernon was three. She considered me a pest.

One year, our school presented a festival. It was decided the tallest in each grade would lead the line. There were four tall, skinny Taylor children first in line, and one Helen, scarcely five feet tall, last in line. Kent, my youngest brother, was not in school at that time.

When Helen was in high school and in the 4-H Club, she entered a room improvement contest. They were to redecorate without spending much money. We shared a room with twin beds. She made blue-checked bedspreads with ruffles on them. Then, she made curtains out of yellow homespun with blue-checked ruffles. Next, she took a barrel, cutting out one-third of the front halfway down, and inserted a stool as a seat. The whole thing was padded and covered with blue-checked gingham. With a few other adornments, she won the competition for the county.

There had never been anything Helen didn't think she could do. She had been a shrimp boat captain, a traveling salesperson, an owner of a restaurant, a meat cutter, a manager of a grocery store, an owner of a sawmill that made skis, a bookkeeper, an insurance salesperson, a Sunday school teacher, and a mother of three sons. In addition, she always reminded me that she had made teeth.

The grounds around her home, maintained by her on a riding mower, were gorgeous, with many blooming flowers and plants. Her friends, like my father's, came from every walk of life: politicians, ministers, poor blacks, rich whites, and just ordinary folks.

Throughout most of her adult life, Helen was a member of the Men's Poker Club, and in her later years, enjoyed gambling in Las Vegas and Atlantic City.

Helen, at the age of eighty-six, left us in the year of 1999. *Angels beware!*

The Turning Point

My brother
Everybody's friend
My mother's favorite child
The tough high school football player, tall, lean, lanky
Nicknamed "Bones"
Kind, generous, tender, always giving,
Expecting nothing in return.

That summer morning, the fog, the convertible, the semi-truck,
The crash! A light extinguished.

The newspaper
Young twenty-one-year-old man, accident victim.

The sister
Three years younger, independent, self-centered, determined,
Headstrong, obstinate.
Suddenly, the light that had gone out caused
The things of the world to grow strangely dim
In the light of things that really matter.

The turning point
God, family, people, sick people, grieving people, young people,
Old people, poor people,
Giving, caring, sensitivity, integrity,
A realization of what really makes a light glow!

Vernon

I remember my older brother, Vernon William Taylor. He was 6 feet 4 inches tall, skinny, and nicknamed, "Bones," in high school. He was very strong, fun-loving, and a real daredevil. There was nothing he wouldn't try.

I remember the time, without permission, we went to pick magnolias. Vernon was about eight years old and climbed to the top of the tree to get the prettiest blossoms. He fell out of the tree, stunned, but no bones broken. When we returned home, not telling our parents about what had happened, my mother said, "Vernon, I was waiting on you to clean out the gutters."

I also remember the day the second wagon ran over Vernon after he fell from the first wagon and had to go to the hospital.

Vernon was good to me. I was three years younger and he would always ask if I needed anything. He would tell me to just use his charge account at the school's snack stand. He also advised me of undesirables, both males and females.

He was only twenty-one on that last, early, foggy morning when he lost his life. My uncle, Sidney Taylor, was riding with him. They were going to work from Ridgeland to Hardeeville, South Carolina. Both worked for my father in road construction. Vernon was passing a car near an approach to a bridge. There was a large, heavy truck coming from the other direction. They didn't make it. Vernon only lived several hours. Sid recovered.

I always thought Vernon was my mother's favorite child. He looked more like her than any of us. My mother was unable to fix his favorite foods, roast pork or peach ice cream, for some months. She never seemed really happy after we lost him. We were never to see that bright flame again!

Vernon, at the age of twenty-one, left us in the year of 1936.

Gray

I remember my brother, Gray Heyward Taylor, named after my grandfather and father. I remember the day a mule kicked Gray in the ear that became infected and he was in a hospital in Savannah for some time.

Gray was three years younger than me. He and I were the third and fourth children of the family. Our parents were so busy that we learned to be independent at an early age. Gray had a gentle nature. He and I both detested turmoil and disturbances.

My Aunt Clifton Carolyn was married to an Englishman. I don't remember the reason, but law officers along with my uncles, Ruth and Lewis, were chasing him. The Englishman pulled out a gun and grabbed my little brother, Gray, who was less than three years old at the time. This was the only other time I saw my mother cry. He took him down the road leading into the farm area, not realizing there was no way out. Gray said he remembered being hidden behind a log. The Englishman was captured and taken into custody. Fortunately, Gray was not harmed. Not long after that, there was a divorce.

When Gray went to college at The Citadel in Charleston, he had an emergency appendectomy. My mother requested that I go to Charleston to be with him. One morning, when he was feeling better, he was reading a *Mad* magazine and I was reading a *True Story* magazine, when in walked the president of The Citadel, General Summerall, a four-star general, with his entourage. We were speechless!

Another time, Gray wanted to go and visit his high school sweetheart. She was attending Georgetown University. He invited a friend of mine and me to go with him to Washington, D.C., as chaperones. We enjoyed touring the city. Gray and Betty later married and had four children.

All through his life, Gray was the one we could always talk with about our problems. He never took sides. He remained that gentle, kind person throughout his life.

Gray, at the age of seventy-nine, left us in the year of 2000.

Jimmy

I remember my brother, James Franklin Taylor, the third boy and fifth child in my family. At six years old, I didn't see anything special about the little fellow that ate or slept all the time. But, I would soon have another sibling to play with.

I wonder what happened to that sweet, passive, towhead-ed, little boy with the big imagination—an imagination so big the four-year-old would tell us constantly about the wife he had tied to the big oak tree to keep her from running away. Sure enough, he would have a real rope tied around the tree.

Jimmy was the most unlikely to be like our father, the most like him in some ways, and the least like him in others. Like him in being able to trade a pig for a hog, a hog for a cow, a cow for a horse, and on and on. Like him in knowing what things would make money, and when the time was right for him to make it. Like him in choosing the right wife, one who'd be willing to go the extra mile to make his life beautiful. Jimmy and his wife, Margie, had three children.

Jimmy was a big risk-taker, but one who considered all angles and consequences. His risk-taking resulted in one successful accomplishment after another. He held leadership positions in countless community and civic organizations, and was well-respected and influential throughout the state of South Carolina. Perhaps that big imagination led to risk-taking, and risk-taking led to success!

Jimmy, at the age of eighty-four, left us in the year of 2008.

Kent

I remember my youngest brother, Richard Kent Taylor, and the night he was born. My Grandmother Gray was visiting us. It was October and cool enough for a fire in the fireplace. Nine-year-old me woke up very early that morning to go to the bathroom.

On my way back to bed, my grandmother came in and announced, "Carolyne, you have a new baby brother."

"Oh no! Not another one!" I said, and went on back to bed.

I remember seeing the large, black nurse, Aunt Mariah, feeding the little, red, squalling infant warm water with a teaspoon. Later, I can still see my mother sitting in my sturdy little rocking chair in front of the fire, bathing the newborn child.

He was the last child to be born into our family and knew how to get my parents to buy him hamburgers, hot dogs, and barbecue sandwiches by refusing to eat anything else. Since the rest of us were married before we were twenty, we all helped our parents to spoil him rotten.

This handsome, young man studied art before he married. Although he was an excellent artist, he did not pursue art for a career, choosing the restaurant and hotel business instead. I always thought that for years, Kent was trying to find himself. I often wonder if he ever did.

Kent, at the age of seventy-nine, left us in the year of 2005.

Chapter 17

My Husband, My Children, and My Grandchild

Ray

I remember my husband, Herbert Ray Wynne. His mother was from Williams, South Carolina, and his father from Havelock, North Carolina. Ray was born in Colleton, South Carolina, where his father worked for a lumber company. He had only one sibling, a sister, Lillian. His parents and sister called him "Sonny Boy," even after he was a grown man and married.

Ray's family moved to Cayce, South Carolina, when he was just beginning high school. He said he tolerated book learning, but loved sports, and excelled in baseball, softball, and boxing. At the beginning of his junior year, they moved to Tillman, South Carolina, and he went to Ridgeland High School and continued pitching ball and boxing. He liked exercise and kept his body in good condition with push-ups and lifting weights. I guess Terry gets her enjoyment of exercise from him.

Ray's father, being in the lumber business, began teaching it to Ray while he was a teenager. In the summers, he worked hard, saving his money. Summer was good for Ray. When the lumber company formed a baseball team, he was their top pitcher and the team began to play and win against other semi-pro teams. Of course, being a top pitcher helps anyone's ego.

Soon, Ray began working full time in the lumber business. It wasn't too long before he began to make some local sales. Being so knowledgeable about lumber, he became really good at sales. The company expanded his sales territory and he had to do a lot of driving and some flying. To be more centrally located, the company wanted us to move to Atlanta. Sadly for him, that put an end to his playing baseball.

Ray's best replacement was watching wrestling on television. Our only son, Steve, began watching wrestling with him and later, Steve began wrestling when he was in high school. Ray went to watch most of his wrestling meets. Our most heartbreaking time was when we lost Steve at the age of 26.

Ray enjoyed our family vacations to Gatlinburg—breathing the clean, cool mountain air; wading in the streams; and particularly eating the giant hot stacks of pancakes with their different toppings like whipped cream, strawberries, blueberries, and pecans.

Ray loved Daytona Beach even more than the children. We all liked the Castaways Motel and were disappointed when it was no longer there. He and I went to Hawaii, but he still liked Daytona Beach the best and continued to vacation there.

Ray took chemo for a long time to control the cancer that ravaged his body until his body rejected it. Then, he had to stay in the hospital. I was there to hear him scream, "Steve! Steve!" Those were his last words. Soon after, he joined Steve in that painless, happy place.

Ray, at the age of sixty-two, left us in the year of 1977.

Diane

My oldest daughter, Diane Wynne Norris, was supposed to arrive in the world on May 22. But, I wanted her to wait until

May 24, my birthday. Oh, why did I ever want her to wait? She waited until June 11!

After waiting three uncomfortable days in the hospital, the doctor said he would have to take some action. Some time later, he came out of the delivery room, told Ray, her father, and Helen, her aunt, that it didn't look like he could save both mother and baby. Later, a nurse brought out a beautiful baby girl for them to see. They asked about me and were told that the doctor would be out to talk to them. For many minutes, they thought I had died. We fooled the doctor, we both survived!

Her nursery was so prettily furnished on a shoestring. Her father made a sort of credenza with shelves on the ends for toys, and doors in the center—an area for blankets and Curity diapers. We painted it ivory to match the crib and wardrobe chest, adding decals of teddy bears. We found an old car seat and my mother helped me cover it in a lovely blue material. The curtains in the bright, sunny windows were white organdy with eyelet ruffles embroidered in blue to match the homemade love seat. Over the chest, a round mirror with a frill to match the eyelet ruffle completed the darling nursery.

For eight months during the pregnancy, a very good friend of mine, Jennie, and I worked on the layette. We made beautiful silk sacques and kimonos, all edged in lace and delicately embroidered. All receiving blankets had hand-crocheted edges and appliques. The little bootees were also hand-crocheted. The very pretty baby had a wardrobe fit for a princess, all handmade and all from a modest budget.

I had insisted we buy a baby carriage. We could move the carriage from room to room wherever we were, and let the baby sleep on the screen porch in the fresh air. Diane was the first baby in our little village near Tillman, South Carolina, in about five years. So, she was the new toy for the children. They amused her, rocked her, and strolled her. She was one spoiled brat!

My brother Jimmy and his wife had a little girl, Celeste, who was just a month younger than Diane. Celeste didn't have much hair and couldn't talk, but learned to walk long before she was a year old. Diane had beautiful hair and could talk, but didn't learn to walk until she was fourteen months old. I was devastated!

Our only source of a library was the bookmobile that came each Friday. We always checked out the limit, five books each. When Diane was four, she taught herself to read. She constantly asked, "What's this word? This word? This word?" Today, she is still an avid reader.

When Diane was five, she received her cousin Mickey's bicycle. She could scarcely reach the pedals. Our after-supper activity was helping her learn to keep her balance on the heavy bicycle she was determined to ride. There were no training wheels then. Another source of pleasure was a slide and swing set that had also belonged to Mickey. Along with a baby pool and sandbox, she had quite a little playground. When she was nine years old, we left the small village and moved to Atlanta.

The highlight of Diane's life came in the form of a golden-haired baby girl, Heather Elizabeth. Heather's mother and father decided they would be happier living apart, so Diane has been a single parent since Heather was a year old.

Now that she's retired, Diane loves staying home, working puzzles, reading, and watching television. But most of all, she loves being a grandmother!

Mother's Day

For today's Mother,
A special time when
Mom's the queen.
Hugs, happy, warm feelings,
Florist flowers, long distance calls,
Cards, gifts, restaurants, "no doing dishes."

For the Mother
No longer with us,
A white rose,
Sadness, memories.

For the Mother
Who misses the
Beloved one who
Once called her Mom,
There is overwhelming
Emptiness.

Steve

I remember our only son, Steven Duane Wynne. After a miserable pregnancy and a prolonged delivery, a little red, wrinkled baby was born. The delivery room was in complete silence. I looked over to the left; the doctor was holding the baby upside down and slapping him on his backside. The silence was broken when I heard the doctor say, "Breathe, please *breathe!*" That was all I was to see of my son until the next day.

After several days of being fed intravenously, bottle-feeding began, but so had pyloric stenosis, a condition that causes severe projectile vomiting. Many medications were tried before one was found that was effective.

Steve continued to be a sickly child. When he was thirteen months old, he spent almost a month in the hospital before they removed his tonsils, although strep throat continued. Finally, the doctor said, "If you can just raise this young man until he is six years old, he'll be fine." I was to remember those words many times. I don't know if it was our move to Atlanta away from the damp, Low Country climate or being six years old, but those words did come true!

I loved his golden, curly hair, though it was cut when he was two; we wanted people to know that he was a boy. He proved this when he was four. Seeing a bulge in the pocket of his jeans, I asked what it was.

He replied, "Oh Mom, it's just a rat, a dead rat."

Steve turned into a handsome, affectionate, but mischievous child. It was Vacation Bible School time. I led the Juniors, with an emphasis on good behavior. Steve was in the four-year-old group. In this small-town church, Vacation Bible School ended with a supper for all parents, leaders, church members, and participants. Each age group went on stage to show and tell some of the things they had learned. While Steve's group was singing on stage, he really showed off. Taking off his belt, twirling it like a rope, he began to sing, "Yippy–yi–yo–ki–yay!"

The audience had a great laugh, but his mother had her greatest embarrassing moment.

Steve always loved people, old and young, male and female, and always had many friends. At age four, his favorite was Little Pete, who would beat on him until he had a bloody nose. Steve didn't like to fight and wouldn't hit back no matter how often Little Pete hit him. After a nosebleed had occurred many times, I warned both boys, telling Little Pete if it happened again, I would force Steve to hit back.

It happened again! There's just so much a little boy can take and so little that his mom can tolerate. I found a wisteria vine; there is no switch as deadly stinging as the wisteria. I grabbed Little Pete with one arm, and Steve with the other. Threatening the little switch and holding his hand, with tears in his eyes, I made Steve hit that cute little towheaded, blue-eyed, innocent-looking playmate. The one on the receiving end of the blows was so frightened that he broke loose and ran under the house as far as he could go. But, that put a stop to the bloody noses.

After tending to Steve's nosebleed, I got out some cookies and milk and we called and called to Little Pete to come out and get some.

His answer was always, "No!"

It wasn't long before Rosa, the maid, came to get her little charge.

After many calls and threats from her, the answer was still, "*No!*"

It wasn't until an hour later, when Little Pete's mother came home from work, that she came to claim her son. She was furious with Steve's mom until she finally heard the whole story and we both had a good laugh about our sons. As they started to go home, Little Pete remembered, "But, I haven't had my milk and cookies yet!"

Several days after I had come home from the hospital with

my new baby, Terry, I couldn't find almost-five-year-old Steve anywhere. Leaving the new baby asleep in the house by herself, I started out for Little Pete's house about a block away. Rosa, the maid, said he and Steve had taken their BB rifles and gone hunting down the log railroad tracks. Now, Steve's father had given him a one-shot BB rifle for Christmas. I was so weak and upset, leaving my newborn alone and having two boys not even five years old off hunting by themselves.

I cut through the backyard of a friend's house on the way to the railroad tracks. In her backyard, I saw an ax stuck in their big chopping block. The yard was rampant with wisteria vines. I picked up that ax and used it to chop about a three-foot vine.

Away down the tracks, I could see two little boys with rifles on their shoulders. After much screaming and yelling, I finally drew their attention. When they saw me, Little Pete began running in the opposite direction, but Steve could see what my hand was holding. He came towards me and soon Little Pete followed.

The tears began rolling down. I didn't say a word until I left Little Pete with Rosa at his home. When that little vine started stinging Steve's little legs, he ran so fast I couldn't catch him until he reached home. The rifle was put away on the "do not disturb" shelf, Steve went to wash up, and the new baby slept on peacefully.

After we moved to Atlanta, out-of-town relatives came to visit. Steve had to give up his bed. After a few days, we drove all of our guests to the airport, where one of them departed. Six-year-old Steve said goodbye, then climbed back in the car. Oblivious to the two guests still in the car, he happily announced, "Well, Mom, we got rid of one of them!"

In the 9th grade, after Steve answered a phone call, he said that he was going to visit a friend who lived several blocks away. It was already eight o'clock on a school night. I told him it was too late to go. He ran out of the house saying, "I will *so* go!"

I got in the car, and when he saw the lights, he ran into the bushes beside the road. I drove slowly, and could see the bushes moving. I called out loudly from the car, "If you don't get in this car, I'll call the police to pick you up."

The teenager got in the car saying, "You'd be just mean enough to do that."

"Mean enough to make sure you're safe," I replied.

After another episode with hubcaps, a probation officer suggested that he was in with the wrong group of friends. We moved, and with time, he turned his life around, started lifting weights, became interested in wrestling, and soon became captain of his Druid Hills High School wrestling team.

When he was at Georgia State University, Steve became active in Sigma Nu Fraternity. We ate and drank Sigma Nu day and night when he was at home. I think this was the happiest time of his life.

Steve began working for the county recreation centers. He always said that his idea of success was teaching a special needs child how to throw a ball. Ultimately, he proudly worked in the Athletic Division of the DeKalb County Parks and Recreation Department.

To add the angels in heaven to his long list of friends...

Steve, at the age of twenty-six, left us in the year of 1972.

Success

Nine-year-old Johnny
for the first time
throws a ball.
You see, young Johnny
is dreaming of being
in the Special Olympics.
That's Success!

Look, there's Mary,
she's special too,
practicing her jump.
Sometimes, it was only
a few inches, but
now it's almost two feet.
That's Success!

And, what about
forty-five-year-old Robert?
He just finished
reading his first book,
Dick and Jane.
If he continues his reading,
he'll soon be able to vote.
That's Success!

Terry

My youngest daughter, Terry Lynne Wynne, was born just before seven o'clock one morning. I was trying very hard to wait on Dr. Pinckney. I didn't like his brother, Dr. John. Natural childbirth had not come into fashion at that time, but without Dr. Pinckney, I was forced to have it and I was furious! Nevertheless, after it was over, I felt fine and had a happy, little, fair-skinned baby with black, curly hair.

Almost daily, every child in the neighborhood came to see her and touch her with their little, dirty hands. We had given away all the baby clothes and baby furniture since Steve was five and Diane was eight years old. I said we'd just stick Terry in a dresser drawer, but her father bought her a crib while I was in the hospital. She was so active before she was born, we bought two high-back Boston rockers, thinking perhaps she was twins.

Before she was born, I was quite active in our church and community. The preacher said he was afraid she would be born in front of a podium. I taught an intermediate Sunday school class on Sunday mornings, an adult Sunday school class on Sunday afternoons, was president of the Woman's Missionary Union, led the intermediate Girl's Auxiliary, and was president of the P.T.A. Now you know why Terry is so good at teaching seminars and public speaking. She began appearing in public before she was born. After her birth, we had a continuous parade of visitors from these organizations. She just smiled and gurgled and let everyone hold her.

She wanted to keep up with all the children and was taking steps at seven months. We moved to Atlanta when she was thirteen months old and she amazed the neighbors going down the sliding board all by herself. When Terry was three, she was so lonely during school hours that we enrolled her in nursery school so she could be around other children. When she was four, the nursery school director asked if I minded if she went into the five-year-old group as the four-year-old group was overcrowded. When she was five, the teacher said, "Don't send her back next year, she's already reading and writing." So, off to a private school, Ar'Lyn Worth, which would take a five-year-old in the 1st grade.

In the 2nd grade, Terry attended public school. We had a distressed child because the teacher resented the three six-year-old children in her 2nd grade class. None of us mothers realized that each of these children was having problems until the end of the year. The teacher told me that Terry led the class in everything but math. I told her that none of us are perfect and that if Terry did her best, then that was all right with her parents. Unfortunately, the end result was that Terry was left with a phobia about math.

In the 8th grade, Terry constantly was ill. The doctor kept calling it a virus. The school would call me several times a week saying she was sick. I would ask them to call a taxi to take her home. At that time, I was the bread-and-butter winner working across town, and couldn't leave work every day to take her home. It was such a dilemma.

Finally, right after Christmas, we reached a crisis. She was having fever, couldn't keep anything down, and rapidly losing weight. She was hospitalized and through tests, was finally diagnosed correctly. She had an ulcer and hepatitis A. This meant complete bed rest, limited diet for several months, and also a homebound teacher. But, before the end of the year, she returned to school and successfully completed the 8th grade.

At the end of the 10th grade, she made the varsity drill team and was happy with her friends in high school. During this time, she was already helping her friends to solve their problems. She had begun her counseling practice. It wasn't until after some years at Furman University and Georgia State University, a bachelor's degree, a master's degree, and a specialist in education degree, that she began to receive pay for this kind of service.

Today, Terry enjoys career counseling, writing, and giving presentations as well as leading seminars. She's unafraid of trying new things or going new places. Her love of adventure and travel has never ceased, and I'm grateful, for we have enjoyed traveling together all over the world to those exotic places with strange-sounding names.

I hope she continues to pursue her many interests and always has a cup overflowing with happiness!

Childhood Comparisons

Rapid transit, expressways, malls, high rises, apartments, and playgrounds
Or duck ponds, fields, gardens, and forest trails.

An overprotected only child
Or one of six very independent, competitive children.

Being enticed to eat by playing games
Or knowing to be on time at the table to get your share of the meal else
to be left with cornbread and veggies.

Riding your big wheel, bicycle, and skateboard
Or riding a pony, a circus horse, and in a goat-hitched cart.

The Golden Arches, Red Lobster, and all-you-can-eat buffets
Or watermelon cuttings, sugar cane grindings, and real pit barbecues.

Amusement parks, movies, television, and cartoons
Or radio, horseback riding, and shooting at targets.

Today, which would you choose?

Heather

When my granddaughter, Heather Elizabeth Norris, was born, we did not recognize the little newborn with her peach fuzz and father's coloring. Heather was a very demanding child, as was her mother, Diane. She wanted to be entertained constantly. I would walk her around the apartment telling her to smell the flowers in the pictures on the walls. She would try to smell everything and still does today.

Not being capable of carrying a tune, I would rock her and sing that old song about "the bulldog on the bank and the bullfrog in the pool." With my squeaky voice, I sounded just like the bullfrog, but it would put her to sleep.

Heather always crawled without letting her feet touch the floor. Magazine page-turning, so difficult for most little ones, was a breeze for her. Not only would she turn the pages, she would turn to the baby food ads indicating she was hungry and wanted something to eat. This child did not like people and would not let anyone near her, not even her beloved Aunt Terry, who became her favorite by the time she started school.

I remember for the whole year when she was two years old, she weighed twenty-two pounds and loved to tell you so. We were amazed at her ability to count and play the alphabet game. At an early age, she developed her own language. Her favorite word was "eni," meaning give me more or do it again. She especially used it for cookies.

We were all apprehensive when her mother was told that Heather would have to have major surgery before she was four. She did quite well with the surgery and has had no trouble since.

From the time Heather was two years old until she was six years old, I had no plants. You see, Heather thought the plants should be able to lie down and go to sleep, so she would bend their stems and lay them down.

Heather's favorite activity was to go outside. She loved nature and started her own "Cluck Nature Club." Its members were her mother, her Aunt Terry, and me. She held weekly classes, read us the stories she had written, and gave us homework assignments. Woe be unto us if we didn't complete our assignments from this young, gifted child!

I remember her 7th grade graduation. This all "A" student constantly went down the aisle to accept scholastic awards.

The summer after Heather completed the 8th grade, she and I took a two-week trip. First, to Daytona Beach—like all the rest of the family, she loved it. Then, on to Orlando to see relatives and Disney World, Marineland, and Silver Springs. And lastly, to my hometown in Ridgeland, South Carolina.

Heather decided that she preferred going home instead of to Ridgeland. I bargained with her. If she would stay only one night, we would leave the next morning. When the next morning came, she asked if we could stay longer. She loved all the cousins wanting to sit by her and wanting her to play with them, loved the Chechessee River house, the boats, and the fresh seafood. We barely made it home on the last day of the vacation.

Heather loves to write. Her poem, "The Season of Our Youth," was chosen as the only poetry to be read at her high school graduation. When she submitted some of her other writings to a national poetry contest, she won both the youth and adult poetry divisions. This smart young lady graduated summa cum laude from Kennesaw State University.

I dearly love this attractive, long-haired, very intelligent, exceptional writer, and grandchild. And thanks to her, this Country Girl who became a Southern Lady who became an International Traveler, has now become a Great-Grandmother!

His name is Rylan!

Afterword
Life Through My Eyes – My Reflections

Carolyne and her reflection.

Shadows

What are shadows?
Are there good shadows and bad shadows?
What are the shadows in my life?
Are they the things I'd like to forget?
That I'm ashamed of?
Are there shadows that I'd like to know more about?
Am I afraid to tackle the opportunity to explore further?
Am I afraid of what I might find out?

Shadows have a way of continually changing.
What about life changes?
I know that my standards and values have changed many times during
this lifetime.
Have they gone up or down?
Are they better or worse?
What about the values and standards in today's world?
Would my parents' values also have changed in this changing world?
What would they have done differently?
Am I forgetting that I, too, am a part of the universe?
What would I have done differently?

Where do I find the answers to these questions?

Even More About Me

Visit CarolyneTaylorWynne.com to see pictures of the people, places, and things in this book and to read even more about me.

CPSIA information can be obtained
at www.ICGtesting.com
Printed in the USA
BVOW03*0535230917
495145BV00001BA/1/P